7
Steps to
Becoming a
Leader

Prem P. Bhalla

GOODWILL PUBLISHING HOUSE®
B-3 RATTAN JYOTI, 18 RAJENDRA PLACE
NEW DELHI-110008 (INDIA)

Published by
GOODWILL PUBLISHING HOUSE®
B-3 Rattan Jyoti, 18 Rajendra Place
New Delhi-110008 (INDIA)
Tel. : 25750801, 25820556
Fax : 91-11-25764396
e-mail : goodwillpub@vsnl.net
website : www.goodwillpublishinghouse.com

Kumar Offset Printers, 381, Patparganj Indl. Area, Delhi-92

Contents

Preface

Within each individual there is a leader waiting to be developed. Yet there has always been a great shortage of good leaders in every sphere of life. People blame their luck for not being able to become a leader. They do not realise that nobody is born a leader. To emerge as an acknowledged leader in one's field one needs to acquire skills and abilities that together contribute to make one a leader.

Good leadership skills can add a new dimension to the life of every person, irrespective of the kind of work one is involved with in everyday life. Within the home, one needs skills and abilities to lead the family towards positive values that make every individual a worthy citizen, who is an asset to the community and the nation. At the workplace there is much to achieve at all levels of activities. Good leadership ensures a happier workforce, besides promoting greater productivity and profitability. In the society good leadership ensures happiness for everyone. The civic services are good, there is discipline on the road, and people move about with greater confidence.

Everyone aspires to be a leader, but few know how it can be achieved. For most people it is a lifetime of hit-and-miss experiences that gradually add up to help a person to receive some recognition. Most people are content as they are. However, the person who wants to get ahead in life strives to acquire the skills and abilities that make one a leader. Life is dynamic. It is forever changing. Each day, every hour and every minute, our life is undergoing a change. Which way we take it is our choice.

7 Steps to Becoming a Leader takes you step by step into the intricacies of becoming a leader. The book will help you understand the essentials of leadership. The skills and abilities that are discussed can help a person become a leader in whatever sphere one is working today. It will also guide you to understand yourself and the people around you better. You can add new dimensions to your life by becoming a leader.

— **Prem P. Bhalla**

Step 1
Leadership in Everyday Life

Leaders are seen leading everywhere in everyday life. In the home, we have the head of the family leading others. Even in the small nuclear family one leads and the rest follow. At the workplace, in every department one person leads, and the others follow. A leader coordinates the various departments to maintain a balance in productivity. Still higher in the hierarchy there is the Board with a chairman, who leads the other directors, each one a leader in his or her own field directing the operations of the company. Even in a small business house the proprietor guides a small group of workers. One cannot think of any activity where a group of people work without a leader. It is the leader who directs and the others work as directed.

If there was no one to lead there would be chaos everywhere. This is exactly what happens when individuals work independently unmindful of others who contribute to a particular activity. This activity could be small, or of a national scale creating wide-scale problems when there is a total confusion because of lack of direction and coordination. Governments of nations fall when the people at the helm of affairs fail to give positive leadership. This happens at every level in the society.

For any activity to succeed it is necessary that it must be led to conclusion. This is possible with direction from an able leader, even when he or she is not recognised as such. By the very action of showing direction, of leading towards a conclusion, one automatically fulfils the role of a leader. Since leaders can lead for better or worst, and since development in all spheres depends upon able and positively oriented leaders, it is necessary to understand how leaders develop and perform. We will move step-by-step to analyse the role of leadership in everyday activities and relationships. One must know what makes a good leader, and why some are appreciated for what they do, while others are not.

WHO IS A LEADER?

A leader is a person or thing that leads, one that guides or directs. A leader is a person or thing that successfully advances in a particular activity and shows direction. Our immediate concern is people who lead. From the definitions it is evident that we have leaders in every position in every field of activity. In simple terms, a leader is a person who leads. The principal activity of a leader is to lead.

What does it mean to lead? To lead means to cause a person (or animal) to go with one, to influence one to do or believe something, and be incharge. To lead refers to the initiative in an action. In the negative sense, to lead can also mean to deceive someone into believing something that is not true or is wrong. This happens when a person knowingly or unknowingly induces others to continue a course of action that will probably end unfavourably. To mislead is also leading.

To understand what it means to lead here is a list of activities that are to be observed in everyday life:

- To guide on a way
- To take or conduct on the way
- To go before or be in the front to show the way
- To conduct by holding and guiding to influence or induce
- To guide in direction, course, action, opinion or something similar
- To serve to bring a person to a place
- To take or bring
- To command or direct
- To run in a specified direction
- To direct the operations, activity or performance
- To go at the head
- To go at the head of or in advance of a procession
- To be superior to or have the advantage over others
- To act as a guide to show the way
- To move towards a definite result.

Some of the activities listed above may overlap with each other. However, the list gives an insight into the finer meaning of what it means to lead in everyday life. Considering the different roles one can say that a leader is a person who has the ability to lead.

To understand the scope of what it means to lead, just take a look at some of the common synonyms – allure, beat, conduct, control, convince, direct, entice, escort, excel, guide, induce, influence, manage, outstrip, persuade, pilot, precede, regulate, steer, supervise, surpass.

The word: leadership refers to the ability to lead. It also pertains to the position or function of a leader, an act or instance where one leads. It can also refer to the leaders of a group. Once again, the common synonyms of the word: leadership make it easy to understand what leadership involves – administration, authority, control, direction, guidance, influence, management, power, and superiority.

The word: leading means being important, being the number one in the field. The leading article in a newspaper provides editorial opinion. A person who is important in a particular field or organisation is often referred to as 'the leading light'. In the same way 'a leading question' refers to a question that prompts the desired answer.

To lead or be a leader is a common everyday experience. However, a person is not easily satisfied by the common everyday experiences and strives to be recognised as a leader at higher levels of the society where the position attracts attention, admiration and praise. It gives a person a feeling of importance and enhances self-esteem.

Think it over...

Leadership is not about being nice. It's about being right and being strong.

— *Paul Keating*

LEADERSHIP IN EVERYDAY LIFE

There is nothing new about a person desiring to be accepted as a leader. Even the primitive man was eager

4

to be a leader. In the interests of personal security groups of people lived together in caves or hutments. Since there was need for collective action, only one person could direct this activity, and therefore he or she was the unquestioned leader of the group. Life may have grown and developed in cities everywhere. However, we still read and hear about tribal people living in remote areas almost all over the world, including some of the most developed countries. These people still follow age-old rites and customs. Education and modern life has still to touch them in a deeper sense. Yet leadership activities are to be observed amongst them almost in the same way as we see them in modern everyday life. It does not matter how they choose their leaders, but they respect and follow them all the same.

Every activity requires someone to do it. When more than one person is involved in the activity one leads and the others follow. None of these workers may be aware of the leader-follower pattern, but it exists. If it were not so the activity would not reach its ultimate conclusion. One would wonder how a lonely daily wage earner working in a faraway field, or one helping in building a road in a remote area, is affected by the leader-follower pattern, but as long as the person is being directed by another individual, there is a leader and the rest are followers. Observe it for yourself in everyday life.

The leader-follower pattern exists everywhere. Observe it within the family. It may consist of only the husband and wife. They may inter-change their roles for different activities, but nonetheless the pattern exists. When the family grows, the children are taught to follow until such time that they learn to lead in their own spheres of activities. In the larger families, there is always the head of the family. He or she is accepted as the leader. At lesser levels, other members of the family play the role of leaders.

At the workplace the leader-follower pattern is immediately visible. There are individuals or groups working at different levels of the organisation. Beginning at the lowest level of a worker we can move upwards to clerks, supervisors, salesmen, managers, heads of departments, directors and to the managing director and chairman. The interesting aspect of the activities at the workplace is that like the leader-follower pattern that exists between the husband and wife, and the two interchange their roles for different activities, at the workplace every worker is both a leader and a follower at the same time. While it is necessary to lead the subordinate staff, it is equally important to follow the directions of the senior management. Even the managing director and chairman need to follow the directions of the shareholders or the proprietors of the organisation.

Like the home and the workplace, the society is also administered by individuals who operate organisations that provide a variety of civic services for the welfare of the society. Even in these organisations the leader-follower pattern exists. Every person fulfils the role of a leader and follower simultaneously. Only the balance between the two roles may vary from one position to another.

The important fact that emerges from this situation is while everyone enjoys playing the role of the leader, few are content to play the role of the follower.

LEADER-FOLLOWER ROLES

Why should individuals look at the leader-follower roles differently even though one knows that everyone is playing these roles all the time? The answer lies in the way we look at the situation. Every follower feels that the leader holds a position of advantage. Few look at the responsibilities the leader needs to fulfil, or the additional effort and the sacrifices he or she needs to make. Their attention is focussed on the 'position of advantage'.

What kinds of advantages do people mostly see in such situations? Firstly, a leader is known to enjoy greater prestige, a sense of pride in showing direction, and a feeling of greater self-esteem. Secondly, every follower feels that a leader is being compensated monetarily, or otherwise, at a higher level in comparison with him or her. This may not always be so, but the follower continues to be suspicious about this fact. Thirdly, the follower feels that the leader has a better prospect of promotion or rising in life than him or her. This fact is absolutely true. Every leader has better prospects for growth. Before a person can show direction, one must know which way to go. Everyone is looking for such people. The solution does not lie in being jealous of a leader, but in learning to develop abilities to fulfil the role of the leader at a higher levels.

The three distinct advantages that individuals perceive in being a leader, guides one to club them together to conclude that a leader is a superior person, and enjoys greater 'power' than a follower. Motivated by the desire to wield power and be leaders in one's field of activity, people adopt a variety of ways to gain power. One would do well to understand them.

MEN AND WOMEN LEADERS

While considering various aspects of being a leader, or learning leadership skills, we cannot overlook how people look differently at men and women leaders. Men have always had the edge of being physically stronger than women, and therefore exerting their influence to hold command. Looking back at the history of mankind, we find that women have played an equally important leadership role as men. The methods might have been different, but the purpose has always been the same. Even in the present age, even amongst the tribal people who are untouched by modern life, both men and women fulfil the leadership role.

In developed countries both men and women are actively involved at the workplace, contributing equally to productivity and profitability of organisations. Even within the home, there is a marked difference in the roles that the husband and the wife play in everyday life. With greater economic freedom neither is totally dependent upon the other. Rather, they play a complimentary role, each fulfilling different roles to maintain the institution of the home. One thing is very clear. Both men and women are capable of becoming leaders in different fields of activities.

SOURCES OF POWER

After the basic needs of food, clothing and shelter are fulfilled, everyone directs their efforts to the need for appreciation and praise, and strive to exert power over others. With everyone pursuing to fulfil this need, differences and conflicts emerge amongst people struggling for their share of power. However, a person who aspires to rise in life needs to maintain good relations with as many people as possible. It is not possible to lead well amidst chaos and conflicts. Every person must understand how individuals seek to enhance personal power.

The most primitive form of power is through show of physical strength. To the primitive man, might was right. Even today, many people are in favour of use of physical strength to exert power over others. How else can we explain acts of grabbing and terror?

In a civilized society the concept of physical strength has changed substantially. People strive to be physically fit to enjoy good health, and to be able to participate in a variety of physical activities, games and sports. Boxing, wrestling, weightlifting, javelin, discus throw and several other games are the examples of creative use of physical strength as a source of power. The use of brutal physical strength is best left to the unscrupulous few. In a civilized society the police and military personnel are entrusted with the responsibility of maintaining law and order.

With limitations to the use of physical strength as power, mankind devised yet another form of power – knowledge! When people gain greater knowledge than others, they enjoy an advantage, and this means power.

Power through knowledge has motivated people to learn a variety of skills, to learn about the mysteries of life and the environment, and by gaining experience to tackle difficult situations. There is a race especially amongst young people to gain specialised knowledge in every sphere of life. This has resulted in promoting technological growth and knowledge, ensuring a better living for people all over the world.

Knowledge is best gained through education, through study and experience. While the desire for power through knowledge has promoted specialisation in every activity, it has simultaneously narrowed the perception of individuals. This is unfortunate. To live a complete life one needs knowledge and experience about many facets of life.

With many people striving to gain power through knowledge, it became possible for individuals to hold positions that attract greater attention and respect than others. This has motivated people to work harder, rise higher in business and professions, and attain important positions in organisations through goodwill and influence. The desire to project an image of importance, people build and live in houses that are larger than what they require. They acquire objects to show off rather than use them. They possess more status symbols than items of personal need.

A certain amount of responsibility is attached to every position. One is able to maintain a position only as long as one can fulfil the responsibilities that go with it. When the person fails to fulfil the responsibilities one automatically slides to a position that is in harmony with one's abilities. It is not possible to hold a position forever.

With the loss of position the influence a person wields is automatically altered.

The most conspicuous form of power that people wield in the present age is the power that comes from money. Besides the necessities and luxuries that it can buy in everyday life, money is often used to shower gifts and charity to impress others. Money and its attributes label individuals and nations as rich or poor. The true worth of money lies in the way it is used. In the hands of good people much good can be attained with money. It can be the stepping-stone to progress and wealth. However, the possession of money does not mean that it has been rightfully or personally earned. It could be inherited, borrowed or acquired unethically. To the intelligent person money is a good slave, but a poor master.

The finest source of power is human goodwill. This can do wonders irrespective of whether one is rich or poor, physically strong or weak, has limited knowledge, or belongs to an exclusive group of people in high positions, or is just an ordinary citizen. This power emerges from a positive outlook towards people. It develops from simple little acts of kindness – a smile, a little encouragement, and giving hope and service to the needy. It is a simple art of adjusting with and liking all people. It normally begins from the home, and is gradually extended to friends, at the workplace and in the society. Human goodwill, as a source of power, benefits others as much as it benefits the person who strives to develop it through continued effort. Getting along well with people is a prized ability. Through it people develop greater personal magnetism. Organisations offer the highest remuneration to those who can get along well with people.

THE POWER FROM WITHIN

The most powerful source of power lies within everyone. However, this does not receive the attention that it deserves. It requires special effort to develop it. The vast majority finds it easier to adopt methods that are swift and help attract immediate attention. These need not be lasting. For personal development one needs to draw from resources lying latent deep within each one of us. Irrespective of one's external characteristics, everyone is endowed with this inner power, which can be developed to work wonders. Once this power is developed, it becomes a part of the individual. It can be effortlessly used to influence the people one comes across everyday.

All great men and women of all times have been recognised as leaders for the power they had developed through their personal efforts. They were not recognised for a single act of great merit. Day after day they were involved in small acts of kindness and compassion that not only benefited mankind but also helped develop their latent inner power. These are the men and women who have been able to eliminate the negativities within them to help virtues shine bright and clear to make them natural leaders of mankind. Everyone can follow their example. One need not strive to do great things to develop personal power. It is as simple as doing little things in everyday life in a grand way. The small things well done will over a period accumulate to help develop the personality.

LEADERSHIP DEVELOPMENT

A majority of people are mistaken into believing that leaders are born, and not developed. Many also believe that good leaders come from prosperous and well-to-do homes. Some believe that money plays a crucial role in making leaders. Nothing could be farther from the truth. Good leaders are made, and not born that way. Money and wealth are media to buy material comforts and luxuries, and have nothing to do with leadership qualities. It is a different thing that good leaders attract money and prosperity.

Good leadership depends on several factors that together contribute to develop leaders. Look at the lives of great men and women who are known to have been great leaders in their field of activities. All of them were common, simple people like you. It is difficult to tell what kindled the spark in their mind that changed their lives to be acknowledged as renowned leaders. We can trace out the crucial moment in the lives of some people. For instance, if Mohandas Karamchand Gandhi had not been thrown out of the railway carriage reserved for the fair-skinned Britons in South Africa, he would never have become Mahatma Gandhi. His life might have taken a different course.

The beginning of many leadership activities can be traced to the awakening of a sensitive conscience – the voice from within that led the person to act. God has endowed everyone with a conscience. It depends upon the individual how he or she develops it by becoming virtuous, gradually eliminating the negative influences that hold a person from development. This is a slow process where people build their lives through little activities that benefit both the individual and the mankind in general. Each little activity helps project a positive image, gradually contributing to acknowledge a person as a leader.

When a person decides to develop one to full potential, it is the beginning of developing oneself as a leader. Similarly, when the person searches for knowledge by becoming a faithful follower, one soon becomes a leader. With each success, and handling of greater responsibility, one rises as a leader. Good leadership comes from personal development. It is a slow process and one cannot afford to be impatient about the results.

OUTSTANDING ACHIEVERS

Generally, leadership qualities develop over a long time, and with effort and experience. However, it is not rare when we see young men and women catapulting into fame and recognition. The recent times have seen many such people, although this phenomenon has been seen in earlier times also. Some of the most outstanding achievers who gained fame and recognition come from the field of sports and show business. Cricket, tennis, badminton, golf and chess have seen many young achievers. It was not long ago when Sachin Tendulkar was known as the schoolboy cricketer. Sania Mirza attained similar recognition in the field of tennis.

Reality shows on television have seen the rise of many young performers who were not known only few months earlier, but soon achieved fame and recognition. It is the wide-scale exposure and publicity on the television that has helped many of the performers build a big fan following.

A few writers who won special awards of national and international importance have also achieved fame and recognition. Even in the field of reporting for newspapers and television many young men and women have achieved fame and respect. Achievements in other fields are not always reported or given much publicity.

Do young achievers enjoy a lifetime of fame and recognition? No. We live in a dynamic environment. Change is a way of life. Nothing is permanent. New records are established in every field. Soon they get old. Then there are people who break the old records to establish new ones. Every individual has certain capabilities. One rises in life in harmony with one's personal abilities. Sometimes a person is catapulted to a position far beyond the abilities. This is common in the fields of sports and show business. However, the person soon slides to the position that is completely in harmony with his or her abilities.

Think it over...

If you never take a chance, you will never be defeated, but you will never accomplish anything either.

— *Anon*

LEADERSHIP POSITIONS

People do not only aspire to attain leadership positions in different spheres of life, but also strive to cling on to them. Although this happens in every facet of life, it is particularly visible in politics. People do not want to let go whatever may be the consequences. While in government jobs and in most business organisations retirement is mandatory after a certain age, but in some private organisations and in politics there is no age limit. The septuagenarians and octogenarians are as eager for leadership positions as are the younger people.

The elderly are not strong physically and may also not enjoy the kind of health that may be necessary to fulfil the responsibilities of certain positions, but their desire for power and the pleasure they derive from holding positions is unquenchable. We see it everyday particularly in the field of politics. To counteract this problem many states and organisations have imposed restrictions in terms of age, or in the terms of office a person can hold consecutively.

Management gurus suggest that in the interests of productivity and progress the term of office must be limited so that the person holding it is able to give it his or her best. This is very true because every person has limitations of creativity and ability. To be recognised and acknowledged a person can put in the very best effort, but it can only be for a limited period because 'the steam tends to run out' as we see it in everyday life. Many organisations like Rotary and Lions that operate on an international scale and have thousands of affiliated clubs, work on the basis of a one-year term of office for president, secretary and other office bearers. This system has its own limitations and problems, but the fixed period of office has seen exemplary activity and progress all over the world.

Even in government positions it is customary to transfer positions and responsibilities to new people and places after a fixed term of three years, or so. This prevents stagnation and helps incorporate new ideas into the functioning of the organisations.

From the individual point of view it is natural to strive for leadership roles. However, it is ideal that a person should provide appropriate leadership for a limited period and move upwards, or out of the position in the organisation. This way a person puts in the best efforts, and depending upon personal abilities is appropriately recognised and acknowledged by the society. One continues to maintain a honourable position in society.

Those who cling on to leadership positions claim that there is nothing wrong with holding a position continuously when the responsibilities are being fulfilled, or appear to be so. They do not realise that it is not possible to maintain peak performance all the time. The efficiency is bound to diminish. Only competition motivates people to keep working well. Another limiting factor is that holding an important leadership role generates pride in an individual. Continued clinging to the position tends to convert the pride into arrogance. This is the beginning of one's downfall. There are innumerable examples in everyday life to confirm this fact. Leadership positions must be handled with care.

LEADERSHIP AND POWER

To be a leader is to have power. Even at the lowest level when a person leads a committee constituted of three persons, the leader should carry the other two along, but certainly has greater power in the group. It is this power that people seek as leaders. It is this power that is intoxicating and addictive. For this reason everyone seeks positions in organisations to attain power. With many people seeking the same thing there is intense competition at every level. Only the best succeed.

To be amongst the best it becomes necessary for individuals to develop leadership skills. These depend upon several factors. We will analyse each factor as we move step by step, and understand how it affects the development of the personality and leadership ability. It is a slow process. Besides knowledge one needs to go through experiences that help convert knowledge into wisdom, and effort into ability.

Earlier education has a marked effect upon learning leadership skills. All schools provide secondary education to prepare the children for further training, leading to a vocation. However, some schools prepare the young people for leadership roles along with providing the basic school education. These schools are well known for the positive influence they have in shaping the lives of young people. Parents go to great extends to seek admission for their children in these schools. The parental influence is also important in helping develop leadership skills.

Despite all other things, the most important factor is the individual. Like all other skills leadership skills need to be developed. This is possible only when the individual desires it. The person must know which way he or she wants to go. One must know what one should achieve. It is not enough only to desire to play a leadership role. The field and the activity must be clearly visualised. A plan must be prepared to take one towards the goal.

> ## Think it over...
>
> There are glorious years lying ahead of you if you choose to make them glorious.
>
> — *J.M. Barrie*

WHERE TO BEGIN?

Whenever young people aspire to achieve something, the obvious question is: Where do we begin? Can you begin from any other place than from where you are today? There is no other place to begin from other than from wherever you are today. Remember the adage: A journey of a thousand miles begins with a single step.

What will this first step be like? This first step lies in strengthening your belief in your abilities. You must believe that you have it in you to reach great heights of success. You must be determined to put in your best efforts to move towards your goal of developing leadership skills. You must gain the necessary knowledge that helps shape good leaders. Problems will arise as they always do. But no problem is big for a determined person. The sky is the limit. You have a long way to go. Let us move on to the next step of understanding what are the essentials of leadership skills.

POINTS TO PONDER

1. To live effectively leaders are required in every field of life.
2. A leader is a person who shows direction and leads one to success.

3. All collective activities depend upon a capable leader to ensure success.
4. Everyone needs to play the roles of a leader and a follower.
5. Both men and women are equally capable to serve as leaders.
6. The most primitive form of power is through show of physical strength.
7. Knowledge is also a great source of power.
8. Specialized knowledge leads people to hold important positions that are symbolic of power.
9. "Money-power" cannot be ignored. Everyone is attracted to it.
10. The finest source of power is that gained through human goodwill.
11. The power from within is available to everyone to emerge as a leader.
12. Nobody is born a leader. One needs to develop leadership skills and abilities.
13. The continued success of young achievers depends upon their skills, dedication and commitment.
14. The power derived from leadership positions is addictive. People like to cling to them.
15. Good leadership makes people powerful. This power must be handled with care.

Step 2
Essentials of
Leadership

All great things are constituted of small components that together contribute to make the whole thing. Leadership skills are no different. Many little activities lead one to be eventually recognised and acknowledged as a leader. Nobody is born with all the abilities that lead to leadership skills. It is possible that some people are instinctively better learners than others, or may be fortunate to be living in an environment that encourages positive development of individuals. Many of the abilities lie latent in individuals and these develop only when the spark is kindled.

There are several abilities that contribute to leadership skills. A leader may not possess all of these abilities, and yet may be recognised as a good leader. At the same time independent leaders may derive their skills from different abilities. Leaders fulfil different roles in a variety of circumstances. One may be good at one thing, and another may do something else well. Therefore, one should not be discouraged if one does not to possess all the abilities. If possible, one must make the effort to develop different kinds of abilities and skills because that prepares one for a variety of leadership roles simultaneously.

Let us now look at several skills that lead one to become a leader at home, at the workplace and in society.

LOVE FOR PEOPLE

Mankind is gregarious by nature. People like to live together. When a person is secluded from the rest of the world the loneliness leads him or her into depression. Continued depression can be dangerous needing psychiatric treatment. Living with people requires skills to maintain good relationships. It has been observed that people coming from joint families find it easier to adjust with people than those that come from small nuclear families. This skill is necessary to lead others. In the developed countries, there has been much economic growth, but unfortunately the family structure has suffered immensely. Due to lack of skills in dealing with people, there is large-scale mental uncertainty. The developing nations are heading towards similar trends.

Everyone does not look at people in the same way. Some are extroverts who love to meet people, and are free in expressing their interest in maintaining good relationships. Such people excel in the fields of selling, insurance, teaching and tourism where it is necessary to deal with a variety of people. On the other extreme there are introverts who are not comfortable with too many people. They are generally shy. They prefer the company of a few relatives or friends. Such people are better placed in careers that require limited interaction with people. We see such people in the fields of research, art, office jobs and writing. There is yet another class of people, the ambiverts, who are neither too outgoing nor too shy. They are in between the extroverts and the introverts. They adjust to a variety of situations and circumstances, and are easily accepted by people.

Individuals have different levels of sensitivity to people. It is important to understand this fact because while the company of people can be stimulating and enjoyable for sometime, over a prolonged period it can be a source of tension. It can also cause emotional fatigue with serious consequences. With this in view, it is necessary that a person must understand one's own level of sensitivity to people in general, or to certain kinds in particular. This knowledge helps in giving direction to one's life.

People are an essential element of the leader's role. If there were no people there would be no need to interact with or to lead them. Therefore, it is essential for a person to know what kind of a role is in harmony with one's attitudes and sensitivity towards people. This makes it easier for a person to seek and work in fields where one can be comfortable and can grow as a leader in life.

Think it over...

Manliness consists not in bluff, bravado or lordliness. It consists in daring to do the right and facing the consequences, whether it is in matters social, political or other. It consists in deeds, not in words.

— *Mahatma Gandhi*

INITIATIVE

A leader can be identified in a group of people when he or she seeks the opportunity to act on a situation. Simply stated, leaders have the ability and courage to initiate action. They have a fresh approach to the circumstances. They look at situations differently.

One would believe that the ability to take initiative should be easy to cultivate. However, it is not so. Everyone is already living in a comfort zone where everything seems to move comfortably and one's mind is at rest. To take initiative, firstly, one requires being creative to take a fresh approach to a situation. Next, one needs to get out of the comfort zone to act in what can be termed 'an unconventional manner'.

People often wonder why is a fresh approach necessary. The answer is simple. If one were to keep doing the things one was always doing the results would be what they always have been. Progress and development depend upon a fresh approach. Therefore, a leader needs to look at things from an altogether different perspective, consider the options available, look at the advantages or disadvantages of each option, and then act.

What exactly would taking a fresh approach mean? To understand this better, observe how people look at situations and others. A policeman would always look at others suspiciously. A doctor looks at situations and people in terms of health. A person in high position looks at people as though they are out to seek undue favours. In the same way, different people look at situations and people with a mindset that has developed over the years, and has become a habit. The leader amongst them is optimistic and looks at the brighter aspects of life. A leader knows that there is always a better way to do things, and acts on what he thinks. The secret lies in positive thinking.

Besides positive thinking, a person needs courage to take the initiative in any situation. A new way must be backed by conviction and readiness for action. This involves responsibility and determination to succeed. It could lead to success, but sometimes it may not. In those circumstances one must have the courage to analyse the circumstances and follow it with measures to correct the situation, and finally succeed. Edison was convinced that an electric bulb could provide a source of light. He made many kinds of bulbs but all failed. Anyone would have given up, but not Edison. After failing for 2,000 times he succeeded. He changed the way people live. He is acknowledged as the greatest inventor ever. People with initiative are true leaders.

COURAGE

It requires courage to come out of one's comfort zone. It also requires courage to take initiative, and to do things that others do not dare to. This courage is not based upon physical strength, but upon mental conviction and morality as to what is right or wrong. J.F. Clarke asserts, "Conscience is the root of all true courage; if a man wants to be brave let him obey his conscience."

Leaders are people who think differently, take the initiative and act with courage. They prove their point through perseverance and success. This does not mean that a leader needs to rush into the unknown overlooking possible dangers. A leader with courage is cool and calm at the time of need, analyses the situation, considers a variety of possibilities, and then steps ahead to achieve what needs to be done. The courage of a leader and the rash and foolish behaviour of the average person are distinguished through the degree of circumspection. True courage comes from reasoning.

In certain situations, as in the armed forces or the police services, leaders would simultaneously require physical courage, but to succeed it would need to be based upon moral courage. Physical courage would not mean a total absence of fear, but would really aim at conquering fear through conviction and a purpose.

PURPOSE

It is not sufficient to take a fresh and courageous approach towards situations and people. It is equally important to see a purpose in the new initiative. Without a purpose there can be no useful action. In a situation a person might say, "Let's go." These two words exemplify initiative and action. However, they do not specify where to go. The statement lacks specific direction. No leader acts without a purpose. We must know where to go, and what to do. Only then will success follow.

A leader always acts with a purpose, a goal, and an objective. In childhood when we learn to play football or hockey we learn the importance of putting the ball through the goal post. In basketball, we learn to throw the ball into the basket. We forget the simple principles in everyday life when we face the adult world. Can anyone win without scoring a goal? A goal is the purpose of the game. In the same way, in everyday life, a leader sets goals for every little activity, and then moves towards them. In a game the opposing team prevents the person from reaching the goal. In everyday life the circumstances, situations and interested individuals work like the opposing team preventing a person to score a goal. Courage and determination keep the person going until the goal is scored.

Irrespective whether the activity is small or large, a leader always works by setting a variety of goals depending upon the nature of work. People work on long-term goals extending over years. These goals are split into annual goals, quarterly goals, monthly goals, weekly goals, and also daily goals. When a person is always moving towards goals one can never be left behind? The person may sometimes not score according to schedule because of particular reasons, but he or she will definitely achieve what they have set out to do.

Goals are not always centred on money. Many activities are rewarded with personal satisfaction and the happiness one derives from it. As a leader when a person attains the goals, it gives immense happiness and promotes self-esteem and personality growth. The kinds of activities one may choose may vary from one person to another, but attaining of goals, or achieving a purpose set before a person brings similar results.

Think it over...

To grasp and hold a vision is the very essence of successful leadership – not only on the movie set where I learned it, but everywhere.

— *Ronald Reagan*

A VISION

The need to set positive goals requires a person to have a vision, the ability to think about the future with imagination or wisdom. A leader has the ability to see ahead, to visualise what would be the outcome of the activities in a given situation. The future may not refer to weeks, months or years ahead, but may refer to the next few moments, hours or the day. It may refer to the immediate outcome of an activity. Imagination refers to the ability to form ideas and images in the mind. It pertains to the ability of the mind to be creative and solve problems. Wisdom expresses the interaction between knowledge and experience.

For a leader to have vision would mean to be knowledgeable, creative and have the ability to assess the situation and act accordingly. One can acquire these attributes through effort and determination.

A SELF-STARTER

A leader is always a self-starter, a person who can act on personal initiative. Once again, we can observe an interaction of initiative, a purpose, a vision and action. A leader does not wait to be told what to do. He or she knows what needs to be done, and acts upon it to attain the immediate purpose.

Unfortunately, very few people are self-starters. Most of them lack motivation. For this reason they fail to take initiative and act. It is never enough to be knowledgeable, to know what needs to be done. If the good intentions remain in the mind and are not acted upon, nothing can be achieved. Without achievement a person cannot be acknowledged as a leader.

To be a self-starter a person needs to be motivated, to be stimulated to act. One must know what is in it for the person concerned. Money is a very powerful motivating force that makes the wheels of commerce and industry move around the world. In certain activities it is not the money but the satisfaction and happiness one derives from the activities that motivate a person. Appreciation by the beneficiaries is a great motivating force to men and women around the world. People will go to great lengths to serve just for a word of praise. Those who are spiritually more developed seek neither praise nor appreciation because they are immediately compensated with an inner feeling of happiness and peace.

ENTHUSIASM

A leader always enjoys a high level of enthusiasm. He or she enjoys whatever they do and take great interest in the activity. It is not possible to succeed without interest or sense of enjoyment and pleasure. To a leader work is not a burden but rather a source of pleasure and growth.

Enthusiasm should not be confused with a feeling of excitement. There is a great difference in being enthusiastic or excited. While excitement is fantastic and hysterical, it is superficial. It is a feeling that passes away swiftly, swinging between extremes of laughter and tears. Enthusiasm is deep-seated, serious and self-controlled. It emerges from truth and sincerity and influences both the good and the bad. Emerson emphasizes, "Nothing great was ever achieved without it." Enthusiasm may initially appear like excitement, but based on wisdom it moves towards serenity.

Enthusiasm is similar to inspiration in that both emerge from within and lead one to action. Both promote creativity and new ideas and help individuals to become better individuals. They lead one to success.

CONFIDENCE

Confidence is the hallmark of good leaders. It is another essential element of leadership skills. A majority of people fail to develop leadership skills because of lack of confidence. They enjoy low self-esteem because of their negative thoughts. They feel they are not attractive. The family background may not be to their liking. An unpleasant past also haunts many. To lead, a person must overcome trivial thoughts that hold a person from growth. Through control of one's thoughts, feelings and actions it is possible to develop self-confidence.

Confidence emerges when a person is ready to face a particular situation. It comes from being prepared. One must evaluate personal abilities periodically. Review both achievements and failures. Always strive to improve upon the past performances. Periodically, the estimates of the personality must be upgraded. This requires a realistic approach towards yourself and the circumstances. Devote more time on activities where you have achieved success. Acquire knowledge that can lead you to still greater success. Try a hand at new activities. Success is the best confidence builder. Keep repeating your successes. Never let doubts cloud your mind and faith in your abilities. Develop new interests. Read books on new subjects. Join a club. Learn to sing, or play a musical instrument. Go out where you can meet new people. Your confidence will grow.

COMMITMENT

When a person is committed to a particular purpose, success cannot be too far behind. Commitment is essential for success. When a leader has a vision, sees a purpose, and sets a goal to attain in whatever field it may be, it is commitment that makes it possible to succeed. The average person expresses good intentions, but does nothing about them. When the person is half-hearted, there is no possibility for success. Commitment comes from within, and provides the necessary spirit and ability to attain one's goals.

Good intentions are an exercise of the mind. A commitment is an agreement to act and produce results. The effect of good intentions cannot be measured. The results of committed actions are measurable. A good leader is different from others because of commitment to a particular cause. In every field of activity people are in search of committed leaders. Success follows wherever they go.

Think it over...

The power of words is immense. A well-chosen word has often sufficed to stop a flying army, to change defeat into victory, and to save an empire.

— *Emile de Girardin*

COMMUNICATION SKILLS

It is essential that a leader be able to communicate well. One may be knowledgeable, experienced and wise, but unless one is able to communicate effectively with others, nothing worthwhile can be attained.

Communication is the act or process of communicating, the imparting or exchanging of thoughts, opinion or information. It also refers to something imparted, interchanged or transmitted. Generally, it refers to the use of speech or writing, as is done through verbal or written messages from person to person, as on telephone, or through facsimile machine or post.

Both spoken and written communication are important. A good communication promotes productivity. People communicate feelings and emotions in other ways also. The presence of people on a particular occasion is also a form of communication.

Communication is not restricted only to the spoken or written word. Much is communicated through silence, when one uses it as a tool to introspect, or talk to oneself. Silence is also used to punish another person by not talking to him or her. This is a common sight amongst couples, or children and parents. Even friends use silence sometimes to settle personal scores.

People also communicate through gestures, clothes and even makeup? Women spend much time in dressing and makeup to communicate that they are pretty. It is common for men and women to wear fragrances that also convey a message.

Body gestures convey more than words. People speak with their eyes. Some convey a message through silence and a smile. Others convey their disapproval without speaking a word. You can get to know when people are happy, sad, angry, disheartened, disapproving, or whatever. Facial expressions and the body language tell much.

A leader needs to communicate positive body language. The level of confidence can easily be gauged from the body language. When negotiating, people cannot read the other's mind, but can gain advantage over others through their ability to read body language. Everyone knows that a good posture and carriage make one attractive. So do good manners and a genial temperament. One is attracted to individuals who smile effortlessly and speak convincingly. People who have their backs hunched, or stand leaning against walls and furniture do not look attractive. The way a person sits, walks, greets and meets people communicates much about him or her.

The face is the index of one's thoughts. The power to attract emerges from the thoughts. Controlled thinking influences personal development and success. Happiness and gaiety attract goodwill. Feelings of anxiety, worry, anger and envy leave their telltale marks on the face. A happy state of mind is important to radiate the inner beauty of self. Men and women communicate in a variety of ways. A good leader ensures that there is two-way communication between him and the people being led.

SPEAKING SKILLS

Speaking skills are a part of communication skills in general. These are especially mentioned because a leader's effectiveness increases with the ability to speak well in public. Considering the importance of speaking skills, it is interesting to note that the earliest book on the subject was written more than 2000 years ago. Speaking skills formed a part of the teaching curriculum at that time. Though not taught as a subject in schools and colleges, public speaking is important in everyday life. Many make up lack of learning by taking classes in later life.

Leadership skills are closely linked with speaking skills. People look forward to hear leaders even when they are not orators. Mahatma Gandhi, Mother Teresa and several others possessed leadership qualities. As leaders they stood high above others. They had risen above personal needs, made outstanding sacrifices and above all else thought from the point of view of the common man. People looked forward to hear them.

Leaders become more effective when they possess good speaking skills. It is also true that a speaker is more effective when he or she possesses leadership qualities. Speaking skills and leadership qualities are closely linked. To persuade people to act on a proposed idea, it is important they are convinced that the speaker practises what he wants them to do. People are always willing to follow an accepted leader. People find it easier to accept a leader when he can speak convincingly to his colleagues.

LISTENING EFFECTIVELY

While still on the subject of effective communication it is necessary to understand that a good leader listens more than he or she speaks. One may be led to think that this is very easy, but it is not so. Generally, people speak more than they listen. This has been the cause of many a failure. One cannot be persuasive when one speaks more than one listens. A person who is not heard immediately gets switched off. That would be the end of acceptance of one's leadership role.

People may be poor listeners because of several reasons. Noise, boredom and fatigue are common reasons for a person's lack of attention and listening, but mental blocks cause deliberate failure to listen well. A very important cause is that while a person is capable of speaking a limited number of words in a given time, one is able to hear several times more. Rather than concentrating on listening one begins to think of possible responses and interrupts, thus causing a failure of communication.

A good leader cannot afford poor communication and makes special efforts to acquire listening skills. Listening effectively is as important as speaking persuasively.

Think it over...

Knowledge is the only instrument of production that is not subject to diminishing results.

— *J.M. Clark*

KNOWLEDGE

Knowledge is power. To be able to do something it is necessary to know all about what is to be done. As a leader, one sets out to do things on the basis of what one knows. Only a very experienced and acknowledged leader experiments with new ideas and concepts. This would amount to taking an initiative to add new dimensions to an activity. Initially, a leader depends upon the knowledge gained at school and college, and through everyday experiences.

A good leader knows that nobody knows enough. If one is to sound relevant in everyday life, it is necessary to upgrade one's knowledge every day. If it were not so we would not have the large number of newspapers and magazines selling millions of copies in all languages and styles to cater to the needs of individuals to know which way the world is going. Earlier, only a few in professions like medicine and law thought it necessary to upgrade knowledge. Today, we need to upgrade knowledge in every field. Even in homes, housewives are forever looking for ideas to run their homes efficiently. Trade journals and magazines are available on every subject. Books are also available to cater to every taste and need.

A leader must be knowledgeable and well informed. Each experience converts knowledge into wisdom. The leader is able to sharpen skills for difficult assignments in times to come.

DELEGATION

A leader always has an eye on the purpose of the activity in hand. The purpose must be fulfilled as well and as early as possible. The leader also knows that four hands are better than two, and twenty are far better than four. Therefore, a leader delegates or shares the responsibilities with others so that all of them together can attain the purpose of the activity. The involvement of more people promotes greater productivity. Sharing responsibility is an essential element of leadership.

Most people avoid delegation for the fear that the person may not do the job as well as one can do it personally. This may lead to failure. In reality it is not so. Given the opportunity to work, most people can do a job well if correctly guided and supported. It might be wrong to leave an activity entirely to a person or persons without providing them the knowledge and support. Experience has repeatedly shown that people perform well under guidance. Once they develop confidence they can handle the responsibility on their own.

It is through delegation that new persons are trained for greater responsibility. New leaders emerge to occupy important positions. Let us not forget that nobody was born learned. Everyone acquires skills through learning, and becomes proficient through practice and experience. A leader has a keen eye for people who can perform. Through delegation he or she passes on the responsibility to new people, and in turn personally rises to occupy still higher leadership positions in life.

TEAM BUILDING

A leader knows that nothing can be achieved single-handedly. Delegation offers the opportunity to share the burden of responsibility with others, thus increasing the productivity and profitability. Besides delegating responsibilities to others, another way of increasing productivity is to work as a team. The four alphabets of the word: **team** can be extended to mean – **t** – together, **e** – everyone, **a** – achieves, **m** – more. In a team, together everyone achieves more.

It is a fact that when two or more people get together to achieve a common goal then each person is able to achieve much more than if one were to do it individually. Think about it. You will appreciate why teams are able to attain more. In every office and organisation people work as a team because they are able to achieve more and also find greater satisfaction in it.

In a team, the members do not work as individuals, but as a group, each utilizing his or her skills to attain the goal at hand. Like a football team, the members spread out, each guarding one's position, and yet moving ahead towards the goal in sight. In a team, while everyone contributes the best, it is the united effort that matters. Since each member of the team can have personal constraints, the work of the leader becomes important in keeping everyone motivated and directed towards the goal. Leaders who can keep a team united and moving are always successful.

A good leader builds a team and works hand in hand to achieve much more than it is possible to do alone. A good team is always an asset.

FLEXIBILITY

When several people are involved in a team it makes it necessary for the leader to be flexible to varying needs and situations. Therefore, it is necessary that a leader must be flexible in his or her approach in every activity that he or she may undertake. Rigidity invites disaster. No problem can be solved if one were rigid. In any activity, the leader is guided by the purpose in hand, and with an attitude of flexibility adopts ways to attain the purpose. It does not matter from what position or angle a goal is scored. What is important is that a goal is scored, and the purpose of the activity is achieved.

Think it over...

The ability to keep a cool head in an emergency, maintain poise in the midst of excitement, and to refuse to be stampeded are true marks of leadership.

— *R. Shannon*

38

COOL-HEADED

Contrary to what some believe there is no such thing as smooth sailing in life. Just as the sea is not calm always, life too is not smooth at all times. There will be problems. They will come at strange times and in odd situations. A good leader needs to face them. On many occasions there will be provocations, some of them may even be serious. It is necessary for a good leader to remain calm or cool-headed on these occasions. It is not easy. It is instinctive to respond to a provocation with anger or disgust. It takes a lot of effort to remain calm under such circumstances. Only a good leader who has acquired the skill of remaining calm irrespective of the provocation can do it.

It is common for a person engaged in negotiating a deal to provoke the other person. The moment the person gets provoked and loses one's temper the game is lost. When the person remains cool-headed despite everything success is certain. That is the hallmark of a good leader.

DETERMINATION

We have just seen that problems are a part of everyday life. A leader has to face more problems than others. At times the leader is over-awed by the problems. An average person would buckle up under pressure and give in. A leader does not give in like that because determination is an essential element of leadership. A leader does not let go until the purpose is achieved.

Determination comes from a definite purpose, from confidence and the ability to handle a variety of difficult situations. Determination comes from the knowledge that one is following the right path and has the ability to reach the destination. Carlyle has rightly emphasized, "The man without a purpose is like a ship without a rudder – a waif, a nothing, a no man. Have a purpose in life, and, having it, throw such strength of mind and muscle into your work as God has given you." A good leader follows this advice humbly.

HONESTY AND INTEGRITY

Leaders are always pushed into positions that attract discretion and power. It is not easy to handle power, however small or big it might be. To be powerful means to be surrounded by temptations. Good leaders rise to important positions but protect themselves from temptations by displaying qualities of honesty and integrity. Most leaders do not possess these qualities because they succumb to human frailties and give in to temptations. That explains the wide-scale corruption in positions of power. It is the honest that truly lead. It is those with integrity who are always sought to shoulder important responsibilities.

The path of honesty and integrity is difficult to walk on, but it is the sure path to success, happiness and personal satisfaction. One little slip and a person could be doomed for life. Once a person is exposed for lack of integrity or dishonesty, a lifetime of repentance cannot correct it. Little acts of honesty may appear to do no great things in a person's life, and may sometimes also attract ridicule from friends and colleagues, but each good act adds up to become a good habit and strengthen personal character. A good leader knows it and follows in the footsteps of great people of all times.

CHARACTER

A leader with a good character stands out amongst the crowd. A person's character makes one unique. It is a valuable possession. Its strength knows no boundaries of colour, caste or creed. The financial status has no bearing on it either. It is such a potent power that when developed in its noblest form, it knows no limitations. It easily overshadows the possession of riches, knowledge, intellect, or genius. All great people have distinguished themselves through their character.

A person's character represents what he or she believes in. It can take a person to great heights of glory and admiration. The character helps to bring out and project the virtues in a person. To develop personal power through one's character means to be dutiful, conscientious, truthful and honest. All the religions also teach us similar virtues. To make it convincing, the simple truths are illustrated with lives of men and women who were perhaps no different from what we are today.

By accepting the principles of truthfulness, honesty and thoughtfulness towards others, and making them a part of everyday life, one adds on a very vital force. This force has identified all great men and women who became immortal through their thoughts and actions.

A person's character is not reflected through a single act of great intelligence, genius, or greatness. It is made of little day-to-day seemingly insignificant actions in everyday life. Every fleeting thought affects it. Thoughts become actions, and actions turn into habits. The laws of action and reaction influence every little action a person performs. A person may not be aware of it, but all good and bad deeds are either rewarded or punished. Sometimes the results are visible immediately. Mostly they are not. However, points are scored in favour or against immediately.

IS RESPONSIBLE

A good leader exhibits a high sense of responsibility towards other people and situations. This is a rare quality. These people are reliable in that they will fulfil whatever responsibility they undertake. These people are mature in the sense that they will take responsibility even when things go wrong. They do not hesitate to say "sorry". One would think that maturity and the sense of personal responsibility would come only with age. One would expect these qualities to show up in later life. It is not so. It has been observed even in school-going children. When parents inculcate the habit of acting responsible with people and situations to their children, they are really helping them to develop into future leaders. One is immediately attracted to these children. They grow up to become responsible citizens with leadership qualities. Good leaders are known to never let down those who depend upon them.

CHARISMA

Charisma refers to the charm that inspires admiration and enthusiasm in other people. The word describes the salient quality that makes individuals appear attractive. It is popularly believed that this quality is a gift of nature or a divine favour. Such people possess the ability to charm, inspire, persuade and influence others, making them natural leaders.

Psychologists and sociologists are particularly interested in what makes a person charismatic. Good leaders have used personal charisma for the benefit of mankind. However, misguided leaders like Adolf Hitler and other dictators have used it as a force for destruction. Charismatic people experience personal emotions strongly. They are enthusiastic and also inspire enthusiasm in others. They believe in what they do, and are not easily influenced by others.

Charisma can be developed like other qualities in human beings. When an actor can act charismatic on stage or on screen, why can't a person develop charisma through study and effort? When people develop qualities that lead to leadership skills charisma emerges from the combination of skills and abilities that contribute to the development of the personality.

POINTS TO PONDER

1. Several skills and abilities contribute to the making of a leader.
2. Special skills are required to build good relationships with people.

3. Leaders look at situations differently. When necessary, they do not hesitate to act.

4. Leaders act on the basis of a definite purpose to be achieved.

5. To set positive goals leaders visualize the future with imagination and wisdom.

6. A leader does not need to be told to perform. Leaders must be self-starters.

7. A leader's enthusiasm makes the difference between success and failure.

8. Confidence is the hallmark of a good leader.

9. People rely upon a leader's commitment to a cause.

10. Nothing worthwhile can be attained without effective communication.

11. Speaking and leadership skills are closely linked.

12. One must first be a good listener before becoming a good speaker.

13. Knowledge is power. A leader must regularly update personal knowledge.

14. Leaders delegate responsibility to enhance productivity.

15. More is achieved through teamwork than through individual effort.

16. A good leader is determined, flexible and cool-headed.

17. Honesty, integrity and character make a leader stand out in a crowd.

18. Good leaders are charismatic and responsible.

Step 3
Building Positive Relationships

A leader is nothing without people. Who would one lead if there were no people? Leadership is all about showing direction, about persuading them to work towards a common goal. Just as it is necessary to have people to lead, it is equally important that there must be people who are willing to be led. This willingness only comes from faith in an individual. Faith is based upon the confidence a person is willing to repose in the individual.

Human beings are gregarious by nature. They desire to live in groups. Even when a family moves into a new area, locality or even a country, it gradually gravitates to a group where it finds peace and security. Human beings are complex, both emotionally and physically. While the environment affects their responses, they are simultaneously influenced by personal feelings and emotions some of which are instinctive, but many have been acquired over a period. This makes it difficult to understand and deal with people.

A leader's biggest problem is not the acquisition of necessary knowledge to move towards a desired goal, but how to carry the people along to support and cooperate in achieving it. Depending upon a leader's skills to build positive relationships with people, one is accepted and recognised as a leader. This is the most important skill that an aspiring leader needs to acquire. A leader rises as high as the proficiency in this skill can carry him or her.

Many factors are involved in building positive relationships with people. We need to understand each factor, evaluate our own personal capabilities as related to it, and then adopt a plan to ensure that we possess the necessary skill to carry us towards the goal. It is a slow and gradual process. One learns through experimentation. Both success and failure come our way. Gradually one learns how to build positive relationships to be a good leader.

EVERYONE IS DIFFERENT

Apparently people look alike. This misleads an aspiring leader to think that the same kind of treatment with people would produce similar results. This is not true. People may seem to respond in the same way, but everyone is different.

Every aspiring leader needs to understand that every person is unique. Scientists tell us that everyone is different because they are born with a variable genetic setup inherited from parents. Everyone has been exposed to different environments. Each individual has grown with different thoughts and perceptions. Under such circumstances how can two people be alike? Even when two persons look alike, as we see in identical twins, yet they are different in their thoughts, perceptions and habits. They respond differently to the same situation.

Hindu scriptures tell us that every person brings with him or her fruits of the past lives. They explain that brothers and sisters born of the same parents, brought up in the same home, studying in the same schools and colleges are completely different because of the influences that they bring with them from past lives. Till recent times this was a debatable issue. Scientists do not accept anything without a valid proof. However, modern psychiatrists practicing hypnotism have been able to get information about the past lives of patients. They have been able to connect present-day problems of people with past lives, making each person unique.

Millions of people have come to this world and gone, but none was like the other. We are surrounded by millions of people living today, but not one of them is like the other. Even in the days to come, people will be different. Why should an aspiring leader then look at them as though they were similar? Why should we use the same yardstick to measure all people? When people are different, why should they not be accepted as such?

In stepping towards the role of a leader a person needs to accept that all people are different, and that they will need to be treated as individuals. It would not be right to adopt a common method for everyone. Nothing hurts people more than being treated as a horde rather than as individuals. All aspiring leaders must always remember this sentiment.

Think it over...

The Lord prefers common-looking people. That is the reason He made so many of them.

— *Abraham Lincoln*

EVERYONE IS RIGHT

It is very difficult for most people to accept that whatever a person says or does is right from his or her point of view. Everyone's behaviour is based upon what he or she was taught, whatever one learnt and experienced until a particular time of life. If a person has always lived amongst animals, can one behave like a human being? Observe children. They will copy whatever they see in their homes. They will speak the same language. They will adopt the same behaviour. This explains the variety of dialects we have in the same language. People coming from different regions and backgrounds have similar accents. To them, that is the right way to pronounce words.

Observe the eating habits. People from different regions and backgrounds adopt similar eating habits and behaviour. People behave in harmony with what they are taught. It would be a mistake to label any response that is based upon learning to be labeled as wrong. From the person's point of view it is right.

Therefore, in dealing with people, every aspiring leader must understand that from the individual point of view everyone is right. We must accept whatever a person speaks or does, as right until such time that we can convincingly persuade the person to understand that there are other correct and better ways of saying and doing the same thing. This is not easy because in suggesting this we expect the person to change one's perspective about something. Change involves uncertainty, and people are afraid to step out of their comfort zones to accept change. This is the real challenge to the aspiring leader. A person must first be accepted with certain thoughts, perceptions and habits, and then gradually be convinced that there are better ways of doing things.

EVERYONE IS SENSITIVE

Just as people are different and are right in thinking and looking at situations in harmony with their knowledge and experience, another aspect that needs the attention of an aspiring leader is that people are sensitive to certain issues, and one needs to be aware of these sensitivities when suggesting any kind of change. When these sensitivities are ignored, people are put off and fail to cooperate or support the efforts to attain a goal.

Every individual is instinctively guided by three basic needs. The first is self-preservation. Everyone desires security. This is possible through good health, a useful vocation and means to live honourably. The second need is to keep one's race going. This is possible through a spouse and a family. The third need is for power, to be recognised and respected. Money plays a crucial role in fulfilling this need. Many people are obsessed with money and tend to ignore other needs. This is too common not to be noticed in everyday life.

One would think that it is easy not to touch the sensitivities of people on these issues, but it is not so. Each need is manifested in small day-to-day activities. Though each activity can be classified under one or the other need, it is difficult for an aspiring leader to understand the finer sensitivities pertaining to an activity. It is only through experience that one learns about these sensitivities, and since experience is gained slowly, one can grow as a leader only with time.

The aspiring leader must always be careful about these sensitivities. In the process of gaining experience and understanding individual peculiarities, it is likely that a person may cause irritation unintentionally. On such occasions the best thing to do is to say "sorry". Seeking an apology hurts the ego at that particular time, but for a person who has set leadership goals this is the easiest way to get over the problem and move ahead. An immediate apology heals the injury and is soon forgotten.

Through experience it has been possible to identify some common sensitivities and ways to avoid them. Let us consider some of them.

Think it over...

Good name, in man or woman, is the immediate jewel of their souls. Who steals my purse steals trash; but he that filches from me my good name, robs me of that which not enriches him, and makes me poor indeed.

— *Shakespeare*

WHAT'S IN A NAME?

Shakespeare simply asks, "What is in a name? That which we call a rose, by any other name would smell as sweet." This is only one way of looking at a name. Most people would not agree with Shakespeare. They are very sensitive about the way their name is pronounced or even spelt. It is agreed that people have strange names, and with millions of combinations the people around the world make it very difficult to do full justice to names without having learnt the correct pronunciation or spelling. Nonetheless, people everywhere are sensitive about the name.

Have you ever noticed the statement that precedes serials and movies? It says, "This is a work of fiction…Any resemblance in names and situations is coincidental and has no bearing with persons, living or dead." The only purpose of this statement is to avoid offending persons who could identify themselves with the characters in the film or serials. Similarly, newspapers and magazines change names of individuals when describing activities and situations that could unintentionally cause offence to the people involved. Such is the intensity of the sensitivity of people where the name is concerned.

An aspiring leader cannot afford to ignore this sensitivity in people. When it is necessary to interact with people, one must learn to pronounce the names correctly. In written communication the spellings must be right. People can also be sensitive about over-writing of names in letters and on envelopes. People in high positions like their position or title to be mentioned with their name. This is a human sensitivity everyone must be careful about.

Goethe simply explains, "A man's name is not like a mantle which merely hangs about him, and which one perchance may safely twitch and pull, but a perfectly fitting garment, which, like the skin, has grown over him, and which one cannot rake and scrape without injuring the man himself."

SPECIAL OCCASIONS

Both men and women can be sensitive about special occasions and milestones in their lives. Have you ever observed how people take offence when relatives and associates forget occasions like birthdays, wedding anniversaries or special celebrations pertaining to their families? People expect to be greeted on special successes, promotions and recognitions. In the same way people also expect the friends and associates to express feelings of condolence in moments of grief and bereavement.

In some leadership roles one interacts with a few people and it is easy to ensure that one does not offend a colleague or associate on these occasions. When it is necessary to interact with many people, as one needs to in some leadership roles, the aspiring leader must maintain the details month-wise so that appropriate greetings can be conveyed appropriately and in time. When a person keeps interacting with many people frequently it becomes easy to remember the names and specialties of people. This way a person grows sooner as a leader.

FAMILY PRIORITIES

Everyone is sensitive about matters pertaining to his or her family. To every individual the family ties are important because that is the basis of his or her existence. Lives rotate around families. The entire society is built on the basis of the institution of the family. Every person desires that the family must be secure; their needs must be met. People will go to great lengths to achieve their family goals. To them, this goal is top priority.

Unfortunately, the intensity of family ties varies in different cultures and countries. In developed countries, the economic freedom has corroded family values, and family ties are weak. In many Asian countries the family ties are strong, and the joint family pattern exists. Despite everything the family ties still motivate people to go to great extremes to ensure family welfare and security. For the sake of love and care individuals have been sacrificing all their material possessions for family members.

The aspiring leader needs to understand that the family is an important priority for everyone, and in one's role as a leader it is necessary to honour these family ties. The moment a leader ignores this important aspect, there will be resentment in the individuals, and they will fail to contribute towards attaining the goal. With withdrawal of effort the leader's work will automatically suffer. Therefore, it is important that a leader must respect the family ties of colleagues and associates.

Think it over...

You may deceive all the people part of the time, and part of the people all the time, but not all the people all the time.

— *Abraham Lincoln*

PERSONAL PRIORITIES

To every leader the top priority is for the group led by him or her to attain the goal that has been mutually agreed upon by everyone. In reality, it should be the same for every member of the group. However, it does not always happen that way. There will be member/s who may have priorities other than that set for the group. This does not happen too often, but does happen occasionally.

This can be very frustrating to the aspiring leader. Sometimes it leads one to lose his or her cool. This could be bad when one of the colleagues is guided by another priority. In such a situation it is necessary for the leader to assess why the person is compelled to divert his or her energies to another priority. It could be important. If so, it would need to be respected in the interest of future performance. This could of course upset the plans of the leader and the group. But it is important that a plan must have provisions for such situations. The plan also needs to have flexibility to cope with untoward changes and variations. In many instances when a person is compelled to divert his efforts because of urgency, the other members of the group share the additional burden, and still attain the desired goal.

Some leaders cope with such situations by building time cushions into the **Plan of Action**. These are not disclosed to everyone because this may cause them to ease their efforts in moving towards the goal.

Only a very motivated group is able to contribute towards a common goal. Others can occasionally divert attention and effort. Therefore, keeping the group in a very high level of motivation is very important, particularly when the goal is very urgent. On other occasions, an aspiring leader should prepare plans keeping such contingencies in mind. That will ensure success for the leader.

BUILDING POSITIVE RELATIONSHIPS

It is possible to build positive relationships only after an aspiring leader has understood the sensitivities of the people he or she will work with. Whatever be the circumstances, these sensitivities must always be remembered. The moment they are ignored, problems will raise their ugly heads.

Once the aspiring leader has understood what to avoid in dealing with people he or she has to work with, the next step should be to understand what makes it easier to work with people. While everyone is different, there are certain things that everyone responds to positively. These are the things an aspiring leader needs to observe and adopt in everyday practice. In the beginning they might appear difficult, but when conscious effort is made to follow them regularly, they soon become habits, and one no longer needs to make a strained effort. They just come naturally.

What makes people tick in harmony with a leader? Every aspiring leader seeks the answer to this question. This question is already partially answered when it was suggested that a leader must not hurt the sensitivities of the colleagues. These have already been discussed. As for the rest of the answer, there are several things that make people tick. Let us consider some of the more important ones.

ACCEPT PEOPLE AS THEY ARE

We have seen that God has made everyone different. Everyone is built differently and gone through different kinds of experiences. Even the sensitivities of people are different. From the individual points of view everyone is right. Under such circumstances, if an aspiring leader wishes the support and cooperation of people, an important step would be to learn to accept people as they are, and not as one would like them to be.

This is more easily said than done. All major problems have always emerged because people found it hard to accept each other as they are. The fair-skinned people assert their superiority over dark-complexioned people. The knowledgeable people assert that others are ignorant. The rich look down upon and exploit the poor. Those in high positions take advantage of those who are not so blessed. Everyone thinks that he or she is superior to the other. This touches the sensitivities of others and they withdraw support and cooperation.

If one were to give up the habit of making comparisons and would accept the other as he or she is presently, the act of acceptance would attract one to the other. Everything else comes afterwards. One cannot work with the other unless there is unconditional acceptance of each other. This becomes easier when each person looks at the other in terms of abilities and qualities that both possess. The first quality of course is that each is willing to accept the other. The second one should be the willingness to work together.

The aspiring leader must understand that the second step of agreeing to work together does not mean that it is a blanket agreement to work to attain all kinds of targets in all kinds of circumstances and situations. Such assumptions lead one to failure. The personal sensitivities are bound to be touched in some situations, and the agreement is bound to break, much to the aspiring leader's discomfort. The leader must understand that the willingness to work together really means the willingness to attain the immediate object or aim in hand, and nothing more. It should have no repercussions on one's personal or professional activities. All efforts must be focussed on the cause that has brought the people together. The area of activity can be expanded once the original object is attained, and when everyone is agreeable to do so.

The concept of accepting people as they are can immediately create harmony amongst people, promote peace and understanding, and eventually increase productivity through development activities. This single concept can cement relationships between neighbours, relatives, friends and even amongst nations. One must follow the concept: Live and let live.

This concept is easy in that it is totally dependent upon the person concerned, and not on others. All that one needs to do is to change one's attitude towards people. This would begin with the simple thought, "Everyone is born different. I must accept them as they are. It would make them happy, and me too." To make this thought a part of your life, just keep repeating it. The sheer act of repetition will make it a part of you. The thought will gradually translate into action, and repeated actions will convert it into a habit, a changed attitude towards people. You will be well on your way to be accepted as a leader.

The only obstacle in learning to accept people as they are is one's habit to try to change others to one's own way of thought and action. The moment one suggests a change or a new activity, it is natural for the other person to go on the defensive and may also cause him or her to be aggressive on the issue. It is best not to suggest any change. Only very experienced leaders can act as catalysts for change. Young, aspiring leaders should wait till they have gained experience to make it possible. Their acceptance alone can take an aspiring leader towards the set goal.

LOOK FOR STRENGTHS, NOT WEAKNESSES

After having accepted people as they are, the aspiring leader should know how to carry forward the team towards the mutually agreed goal. This is possible only when everyone contributes towards the attainment of the goal through his or her personal abilities. As the leader, one must be well acquainted with these abilities. To know about them the leader must seek the information from the colleagues who support him for the cause. Seek to know the strengths of each colleague. It is not that the persons would be without weaknesses, but few like to think of them, and even fewer who would like to disclose them to others. It would be useful for the leader to also know about the weaknesses. However, this information will need to be collected through personal observation, and not through enquiry.

The best of leaders around the world have attained success by accepting people as the most important asset, and by motivating them to contributing the best of their abilities to the cause in hand. This cause could be small or big, depending upon the situation and the circumstances, but the principle of attaining success is just the same. The aspiring leader works on a smaller scale. The established leader works on a larger scale, and also in several fields simultaneously. That is the only difference.

While the aspiring leader must begin by utilising the strengths of the team members, over a period the weaknesses must be observed. These could sometimes act as obstacles to the attaining of a goal. A good leader would not only be satisfied by knowing the weaknesses, but would also help the colleague to get over them. Building people is part of effective leadership.

APPRECIATE PEOPLE

Nothing motivates people more than appreciation. Observe how parents motivate children. They will repeatedly remind the child, "You're a good child. Why not put your toys in place?" "As a good child you must be in time for school." The appreciation keeps the child doing whatever is desired. Scold the child, and he will revolt.

The aspiring leader could have no better tool to build positive relationships with people than appreciation. It costs nothing, but achieves much. Parents teach their children through appreciation. A husband takes his wife out to dinner to appreciate her efforts in building a home. The wife hugs the husband in appreciation. At the workplace all kinds of incentives are given in appreciation. Outstanding workers are given status symbols by way of special positions, gifts are given when special targets are achieved, promotions are given to those who are responsible, and of course financial benefits are always welcome to express appreciation for good work.

Even in everyday life we see participants in contests being offered 'Certificates of Appreciation' and prizes for outstanding ability. Guest speakers are given recognition through mementos or tokens of appreciation. In many cities it is common to see organisations honouring citizens who have contributed towards the development of the city. Even at the national level there are a variety of awards in different fields of activities through which the government honours outstanding ability.

The aspiring leader must learn the art of sincere appreciation. One can begin simply by adopting the habit of saying, "Thank you" for every favour done. It does not matter how small the favour, saying "Thank you" is very important. The expression of gratitude assures the other person that his or her work is being noticed and appreciated. The aspiring leader will do well to remember that the appreciation must be sincere and must come from the heart. There are too many people who move a step ahead, and besides expressing gratitude compliment people on their appearance, the handwriting, the style of working or doing a variety of other things. This is effective appreciation when it is sincere.

There are some people who use a variety of adjectives to shower compliments on others, but do it so lavishly that it is immediately apparent that the words lack sincerity. This could have a negative effect. Such compliments are more of flattery than appreciation.

To appreciate people a leader must listen to them, take interest and reach out to them whenever necessary. The leader shares enthusiasm with others. Whoever aspires to greater success must use appreciation to motivate people all the time. Appreciation fulfils an inner desire in all people, and they reciprocate the gesture by performing better. It soon becomes a two-way activity. The leader appreciates the team, and in response the team appreciates the leader through greater productivity and contribution to attain the target. The best of leaders have always used appreciation as the greatest motivating force known to mankind. People always respond to it.

> **Think it over…**
>
> It is one of the most beautiful compensations of life that no man can sincerely try to help another without helping himself.
>
> — *Shakespeare*

HELP PEOPLE

A step ahead of appreciation is to offer help so that the team moves ahead. When a leader asks the colleagues, "Can I help you?" he makes it known that besides his own responsibilities he is willing to share his abilities to fulfil others' responsibilities. They may not ask for help, but in their mind they know where to go when they need it. The leader has built goodwill well ahead of having to share abilities.

A good leader keeps an eye on everyone and helps the person who lags behind. A little support helps keep up the pace of activity. The other members of the team also pitch in their support. This makes the work easier and targets are achieved as scheduled.

The offer of help and support need not be restricted to colleagues and members of the team, but also to people in general. No action goes without an appropriate reward. With every service, one builds goodwill. This helps a person grow as a leader.

When a leader offers support there are some people who may take undue advantage to seek special favours. The leader must know where to draw a line and not hesitate to say "no" to such requests. That helps maintain discipline within the group. To judge situations a leader must always ask, "Will this help me get closer to our mutually agreed goal?" Do whatever it takes, to take one towards the goal. That will help maintain mutual goodwill.

Think it over...

Never does the human soul appear so strong and noble as when it foregoes revenge, and dares to forgive an injury.

— *E.H. Chapin*

FORGIVENESS

While dealing with people every leader is faced with the situation when he or she feels let down by one or more people responsible for attaining the goal. The frustration prompts most people to respond with anger. To most people it appears natural. However, it achieves nothing. Both the leader and the people concerned have nothing to gain. It would be far better to analyse the cause for these people letting down the team. Show concern. Ask them why did they not seek support when it was offered to them? Tell them how they can improve upon their performance. Tell them that you are expressing concern because they were part of a team. Yet give them the benefit of doubt. Forgive them for their lapses.

It is easy to preach forgiveness, but difficult to practise it. Chesterfield said, "Little, vicious minds abound with anger and revenge, and are incapable of feeling the pleasure of forgiving their enemies." Yet Herbert warns, "He that cannot forget others, breaks the bridge over which he himself must pass if he would ever reach heaven, for every one has need to be forgiven."

The aspiring leader would gradually learn that there is more to gain through forgiveness rather than through anger and revenge. Forgiveness helps build positive relationships. That is what every leader ultimately aims to achieve.

THOUGHTFULNESS OF OTHERS

If one were to sum up all that has been suggested to aspiring leaders about building positive relationships with people, it could simply be said, "Be thoughtful of others." Thoughtfulness combines all the virtues that help win the support and cooperation of others. To be thoughtful of others at all times requires the aspiring leader to be a virtuous person who practises truthfulness and honesty. The leader needs to have complete self-control and be fair to everyone at all times. Such people are known for their character, and seek the support of their conscience whenever in doubt. They know that it is God who speaks to them through the conscience.

Irrespective of the faith they followed, all great leaders have drawn strength from God. They have seen God in the common man. In serving him through thoughtfulness they served God. In return they were rewarded with greater strength and a purpose to live. Doddridge advises, "He is the wisest and happiest man, who, by constant attention of thought discovers the greatest opportunity of doing good, and breaks through every opposition that he may improve these opportunities."

In learning to be thoughtful towards others at all times the aspiring leader acquires the mantra to build positive relationships with all kinds of people, and move ahead as a leader.

POINTS TO PONDER

1. A leader's principal responsibility is to guide and lead people.
2. People look alike on the outside, but are different inside.
3. Everyone is right from his or her point of view.
4. Everyone is guided by personal sensitivities.
5. People are sensitive to the way their name is spoken or spelt.
6. To most people some occasions are very special.
7. Irrespective of the time men and women spend at work and other activities, everyone is sensitive about family priorities.
8. When required to make a choice, people give preference to personal priorities.
9. Positive relationships can only be built when one is aware of personal sensitivities.
10. One must accept people as they are, and not as one would like them to be.

11. To build positive relationships one must look for others' strengths, and not weaknesses.

12. Nothing motivates people more than appreciation.

13. People cannot help liking you when you offer to help them.

14. In time of need a leader must try the unfailing magic of forgiveness.

15. Leaders build positive relationships by being thoughtful of others.

Step 4
Using Other's Skills

Leaders work with people. They serve people. To fulfil needs and serve people every leader seeks the support of others. A leader who can seek and receive the maximum support and cooperation is acknowledged and recognized as the best leader.

A good leader knows that a person is nothing without the support and cooperation of the colleagues who share a common goal. The leader also knows that four hands are better than two, and that ten hands can perform much larger tasks. The leader also knows that the secret of success depends upon how well one is able to keep those who give support happy. This is not an easy thing to do. If it were, we would never be short of good leaders. Unfortunately, it is not so. Good leaders are hard to find. At all times, one ability that has contributed the most towards making a person earn a higher salary in every field of activity is the ability to get along well with people.

Getting along well with people is one thing; making them cooperate, work and serve others is quite another. This requires special knowledge and skills. All leaders need to learn and use it. We have already discussed how to develop better relationships with people. As the next step we need to learn how to make people cooperate and support the leader to enhance productivity and attain goals. This depends upon several factors. Let us consider them one by one.

ETIQUETTE AND MANNERS

The society is based upon civilized behaviour amongst people. Although circumstances vary from one region to another, and also between different countries and cultures, mankind has adopted certain unwritten rules of behaviour amongst each other. With the level of literacy improving and with a better level of education, there is greater refinement in behaviour within the society. It is also not unusual for different communities to have their own customs based upon local traditions and past experiences. A vast majority is sensitive and sentimental about following these customs and traditions.

To make it easier for everyone to understand the situation well, the society has adopted certain unwritten guidelines based upon accepted customs and traditions. These help create harmony in human relationships. These guidelines are not in the form of a legal document. They have come into use through innumerable suggestions, conveniences and refinements. Through suggestions people have acted, and with repetition these actions have become customs. These guidelines are not instinctive. Therefore, they need to be cultivated. They require a deliberate effort to learn and use in everyday life. These customs reflect good manners. These eventually transform into etiquette.

The need for harmony in relationships makes it necessary that one must be thoughtful towards everyone. This comes from care and consideration for others. The actions of a thoughtful person are based upon the answer to a simple question: "Is it fair to all concerned?" If the answer is "yes", the person goes ahead. If not, the direction is changed. Good etiquette and manners are not only relevant when one is performing the role of a leader, but are equally significant in shaping the personality of a person.

Parents take great care in teaching good behaviour to their children. They send them to good schools so that they can be shaped into ideal citizens. Everyone desires good interactive skills. However, somewhere down the line some people find self-restraint stifling and deviate to give vent to their instincts rather than follow man-made code of conduct. This leads to undesirable actions and behaviour, and sometimes, even crime. An aspiring leader needs to understand that to be accepted by people one needs to follow the code that is based upon the concept: "welfare of everyone", and has been adopted through practice over a long period.

Although adopted as an unwritten code of conduct, the importance of good etiquette and manners has prompted people to write innumerable books on the subject suggesting the best behaviour within the home, amongst friends, at the workplace, and in the society. Since one spends a large part of the day at the workplace one comes across articles and books on the subject frequently to ensure good behaviour and interaction amongst people. Some people may consider good etiquette and manners trifling and insignificant. Yet experience shows that it is people with good etiquette and manners that move ahead. They are easily accepted everywhere. An aspiring leader cannot ignore this vital need to build good relationships with people.

TEAM BUILDING

It is not possible for a person to perform beyond certain physical constraints. When the task in hand is big, to perform it effectively, it will be necessary to seek the support of others. Instead of one person, there would be the need for a team constituted of two or more people. The leader of the team would show direction to the team members. As we have seen earlier, every person is unique, is different and has personal sensitivities. This makes it difficult for an aspiring leader to understand how a person will respond in a given set of circumstances. One thing is sure. Each member of the team would respond differently. This makes leading a team difficult.

When leading a team, the leader will need to use all the skills. For example, to inspire confidence and enthusiasm in the team, the leader will personally need to be confident and enthusiastic. The leader must completely understand the purpose of the task in hand before it can be communicated to the team. To be able to do so the leader will need the best of communication skills. A vast majority fails on this account. In some circumstances the written skills are important, but in majority of the cases good speaking skills are required. Even the body language should inspire confidence in the team. The team must be convinced that the leader is sincere and committed. The dedication and commitment in the leader inspires these qualities in the team.

A leader needs to understand that when the team is well led, it performs better than the performance of the individual members put together. For this reason the four letters of the word: team together is taken to mean:

T – Together
E – Everyone
A – Achieves
M – More.

Why should this be so? How can the performance of a team be better than the performance of the members of the team? Who contributes towards the additional performance? This fact is explained by Napoleon Hill in his famous work: The Law of Success. He calls the phenomenon as the Law of the Mastermind. According to him when two or more persons get together to attain a common goal, both are endowed with more power than each could wield individually. We see the practical application of this law in everyday life.

Have you ever observed that when a young man and woman get together in marriage, suddenly they become more responsible and focused in life? Have you observed that a partnership firm functions better than a proprietorship business? In the same way, can you understand why companies grow when a well-focused Board of Directors leads them? Organisations grow and develop when a good team leads the affairs.

The success of the leader depends upon his or her abilities to form a good team and to lead it well. This requires a deep understanding of human nature. This comes slowly through greater knowledge and experience. The aspiring leader will do well to acquire it to succeed in attaining the goal.

THE NEED FOR DELEGATION

Who has not seen a self-employed shopkeeper? He plays many roles simultaneously. He is the purchase manager, the sales manager, the accountant and also the shop assistant and public relations manager – all in one! Because of the size of his operations and economic constraints he needs to personally fulfil many responsibilities. This is true not only of a shopkeeper but that of every person setting out to work. However, when the work expands and cannot be handled by a single person, there is the need to delegate some of the responsibilities to others, to ease the workload.

Perhaps the first responsibility the shopkeeper may delegate to another is to hire a shop assistant who can help open and pack cartons, display goods, and in general help the owner. The next step would be to hire a sales assistant to help attend customers and also build good public relations to create goodwill for the business. Still another step ahead would be to hire a purchase assistant to help procure items from different wholesalers to ensure that a wide variety of items are available in the store. The shopkeeper, who started as an individual worker, may gradually lead a group of assistants performing different tasks on his direction. Together they form a group or a team. We can observe this in any field of activity. In each case an activity starts with a single person, but is soon performed by a group of people, each helping in one way or another.

What would have happened if the shopkeeper decided to remain a loner? Firstly, the business would never have grown. After a short period of growth it would reach a point of stagnation, and then a gradual decline. Secondly, with growing age, the shopkeeper would not be able to cope with the work, and would suffer from stress, fatigue and maybe sickness. Finally, to cope with the situation, the shopkeeper would sometimes need to close the shop. This would encourage customers to move to other sales outlets.

It is not that people do not understand these simple things. They do. Yet they do not delegate responsibility because of certain fears. A common fear is that the person may not be able to perform as well as one would like to. This is anticipating failure even without having delegated a responsibility. Going back to the shopkeeper, if he hired an assistant to handle products as they come, or to display them, in what way would he fail? May be he would not be able to display the products well. Initially, the shopkeeper can personally guide and help. It may not completely reduce his work, but to some extent it would. In the same way, if he were to hire a sales assistant, while he could personally attend to billing, the assistant could help in providing and packing the items. Think of the benefits at rush-time. The customers would appreciate better service and the personal attention of the shopkeeper. To ensure that the assistants perform, the shopkeeper will need to supervise and guide them, but with them around he would have more time to attend to customers and also plan future growth of the business.

Another common cause for not delegating responsibility, particularly in offices and in factories, is the fear that the person may become a competitor rather than one who supports a particular activity leading to a goal. In due course of time the person may usurp the position displacing one who delegated the responsibility. This may happen if one were to delegate responsibility, and personally do nothing. However, if one were to delegate a part of the responsibility that could be fulfilled by a person of lesser skills and ability, and would personally get engaged in responsibility that need skills and abilities that come from greater experience, thus increasing productivity and profitability, there would be nothing to fear. The person thus increases productivity. In the process new people are trained to handle that particular activity over a period, and the person rises to the next higher position, making place for one who deserves it.

Another reason for not delegating responsibility is the fear that the person may not be able to maintain deadlines, and being let down at the last minute. This may require the person to adopt crisis management. This would only happen if the work is delegated and forgotten, and not followed up. That would defeat the very purpose of delegation.

Every aspiring leader needs to understand that not delegating responsibility will leave him or her a dwarf leader. If one desires to grow in leadership skills one needs to learn the art of effective delegation. The secret of becoming a great leader is not in doing everything well oneself, but in choosing the right people to do the right jobs, and leading them to success.

EFFECTIVE DELEGATION

How does one ensure effective delegation? Where
does one find the right people? Every aspiring leader
searches answers to these questions. Before one can
effectively delegate responsibility to others it is important
that one must be able to perform that particular activity
personally, or must know how it can be performed. The
leader should never consider any activity too small or
belittling to do personally. The leader should never
consider any activity below his dignity to perform. If one
does, it will send out negative messages to the person
assigned to fulfil that activity, inviting failure even before
one has begun.

Before delegation the leader must understand that
it involves passing some of the responsibility and authority
to others, while still being accountable for the results. The
leader cannot ignore that accountability is an integral part
of being a leader. Therefore, delegation always involves
a certain amount of risk. To keep this risk within safe limits
one needs to adopt the following steps:

- **Assess the task in hand.** The first step should
  be to identify what needs to be done, and what is
  the timeframe. Can the task be broken up into
  smaller activities, together contributing to attain a

74

goal? What are these activities? What are the risks involved in delegating these activities to other colleagues?

- **Assess the people who can support you.** The next step should be evaluating the performance of the people who can support you. Are you aware of their skills and abilities? Can you match some of these skills and abilities to the activities you have identified? Can the persons fulfil these in the timeframe?

- **Discuss the activity.** Next, you need to tell the person why you consider him or her worthy of the responsibility. Does the person know what is the ultimate goal? Is the person aware how his or her contribution is going to affect the goal? Does the person know that periodic evaluation and reporting are part of the responsibility?

- **Keep a check on the activities.** To ensure success every leader must keep a check on how the members of the team are performing. Is everyone reporting the progress? Is the progress satisfactory? Will it be possible to maintain the timeframe? If there were any problems, have they been suitably addressed? The answers will ensure that the work is progressing as per schedule.

- **Do not panic.** When things go wrong, as they will sometimes because of reasons beyond control, do not panic. A leader needs to remain cool, particularly when a crisis is brewing. Call a meeting of the team. Assess the problem realistically. Jointly agree on remedial measures. Re-assign responsibilities, if necessary. As the leader, accept responsibility for everything.

- **Congratulate the team for success.** In the end convey your gratitude to every member of the team for his or her contribution in attaining the goal successfully. This will ensure better performance the next time.

SHARING GOALS

No leader can succeed without definite goals. Setting goals is to know your destination. One who does not know the destination is only moving. When you do not know where you are going, you reach there – nowhere!

We practise goal setting in school. Unfortunately, one soon leaves behind whatever one learns in school, probably thinking that it may not be applicable in adult life. At school, the teachers spread out the syllabus over the session so that the subject could be covered within the time. The curriculum is covered in a year, and one moves to the next class.

While we remember the three Rs we learnt at school, we overlook the concepts that are used to teach us. We forget that we would not reach the class late for the fear that we may be refused entry. We forget that we had set goals before us to complete the work during the academic session. As adults we forget how important goals are to each one of us.

To be useful a goal must be:

- **Specific and measurable**. If it is not, it cannot be a goal.

- **Challenging**. If it were not challenging, it would not be worthwhile.
- **Achievable**. If it cannot be achieved in particular circumstances, it can be counter productive.
- **Time-bound**. If it were not time-bound one would never be motivated to achieve it.
- **Shared**. If it were not shared with those who are concerned with it, it would be difficult to attain it.

It is essential that the goal must be written down and shared with all those involved in attaining it. It would be better if the sharing process begins as early as the moment when a project or activity is conceived, and the team to attain it is agreed upon. When every member of the team is involved with the details of the goal, each person feels more responsible towards attaining it. This way the chances of a member letting down the team are eliminated.

It would be necessary to set all kinds of goals. There would be long-term goals and short-term goals. Depending upon the activity there will be need for annual goals, quarterly goals, monthly goals, and also weekly goals. These would ensure success at every step.

At the workplace, it is usual to adopt product goals to ensure quality at every step. There would also be operational goals for proper utilization of the workers' skills. Consumer goals ensure happy consumers through better products and services. Besides these there are secondary goals that arise from current operations. All these goals are necessarily shared goals, and to attain them everyone in the team must be involved.

Goals need to be set for every aspect of one's life. While it is commonplace to use goals at the workplace, it is equally important to use them at home where the family must share them to have an efficient home. This ensures discipline within the home, and provides an opportunity to the children to learn values of life. Even in everyday life one does well to adopt goals, share them with the family, friends and others, and live a successful goal-oriented life.

> **Think it over...**
>
> It is not enough to aim; you must hit.
>
> — *Italian proverb*

GOALS AND PLANNING

Once the goals are set the next obvious step would be to plan how to attain these goals. A good **Plan of Action** is the ideal way to achieve what one has set out to do. Most aspiring leaders prepare a plan and hand it out to the team members to execute. This does not always produce the best results. It would be preferable to have the team members participate in the planning process also. The leader would need to be careful because some team members could be more aggressive than others, and may dominate the planning activities. To ensure that everyone gets a fair share in the planning process, the leader would need to offer the opportunity equally to everyone, and also to make sure that nobody dominates. This is a tricky situation, but in the interest of success, the leader must be careful about it.

The **Plan of Action** would need to have two components – the macro plan that sets overall goals, and the micro plans that defines short-term or day-to-day goals and activities. It would be appropriate for the team members to share responsibilities at this stage. The leader would have to ensure that everyone's skills and abilities are used for the benefit of the project in hand. Once again, some of the team members may seek easier work or that which would highlight their contribution rather than the overall success of the project. The leader would need to intervene and hand out responsibilities to ensure the best results. The leader must not only be fair, but also appear to be so.

GOALS AND PRIORITIES

At the planning stage it would also be appropriate for every team member to be aware of the priorities of different components of the project in hand. It is not enough just to complete one's share of work within the timeframe. It is equally important that the priorities must first be defined, and thereafter be followed to ensure that no member of the team feels let down or any aspect of the project suffers. In general, there will be three kinds of priorities:

1. **Priorities of time**. Some things must be completed within the specified time.
2. **Priorities of importance**. Some things are more important than others and must be attended to earlier.
3. **Priorities of time and importance**. Some things are both time-bound and important.

When all the team members know the priorities of the smaller goals, and adhere to them success will be ensured.

MOTIVATION

A leader needs to motivate the members of the team to perform consistently to attain the goal. To motivate means to keep arousing the interest of the team members in the goal. It would also aim at ensuring that the person continues to be enthusiastic about the goal. Those in the field of selling need to be highly motivated at all times.

All forms of motivation aim at changing human behaviour, even though it might only be for a short while. We already know that human beings generally resist change, and therefore motivating people is not an easy task. Yet we see the roadside vendor attracting people to listen to him and buy his ware. We also observe large-scale motivation in offices and factories where workers are encouraged to increase their productivity. The ability to motivate team members is a quality that is immediately recognized in a leader.

Every aspiring leader would like to know what motivates people. To get an answer to this question one should observe how advertisers woo prospective customers through advertisements in the press, trade journals, radio and on television. These advertisements appeal to the weaker side of human nature. While on one hand people resist change, on the other hand they succumb to an intelligent appeal that touches a secret need in their mind.

Whatever is the weaker side of human nature? This is none other than the three instinctive needs – the need for self-preservation, the need for reproduction or carrying on humanity and the need for self-esteem or power. In the modern age, money is a part of the third need. It is commonly used to motivate people. Those who aspire to change people use subtle ways to influence them just as the advertisers specialize in this field of touching people emotionally.

The instinctive need for self-preservation includes the need for food, clothing, housing and healthcare. The primitive man had these needs just as the modern people have need for them. However, over the years mankind has intelligently manipulated these needs to introduce new products and services, giving rise to innumerable smaller needs, which have provided an opportunity to millions of people to fulfil them.

The instinctive need for reproduction or carrying on humanity includes the need for a family, a home and children, and the need for their nutrition, education, healthcare and safety. This single need has created opportunities for hospitals, schools, colleges, universities and other needs like books, libraries, etc. Generally, people are so concerned about family needs that advertisers exploit them blatantly.

The need for self-esteem and power initially meant the use of physical strength as a source of power, but it has now refined into other forms like living in big homes, buying luxuries and holding positions that attract respect and honour. Money is a new symbol of power. Everybody wants it because it increases one's purchasing power and ability to buy luxury items to flaunt before others. However, money is a good slave but a poor master.

MOTIVATING THE TEAM

The next obvious question is: How does motivation work? Motivation aims at touching the emotions and feelings of people. If a leader can touch a person emotionally, there is immediate motivation. This comes from the promise of fulfilment of a need.

An aspiring leader needs to ensure that he or she uses positive ways to motivate the team members. The leader could touch a person in a negative way by arousing greed. All corrupt practices do this precisely. By encouraging greed people indulge in malpractices. One can also motivate a mob to shout and destroy through a negative suggestion that touches the emotions. Even good people are known to behave irrationally in a mob. It takes some time before the negative influence wears off.

The most popular way to motivate people used by business houses and organizations is through money. Attractive pay packages including perks like a house, a car, and amenities like free healthcare and an annual holiday package for the family are popular forms of motivation. In everyday practice it is common to see business houses offering a variety of incentives to consumers, retail and wholesale stores and their own personnel.

How does an aspiring leader put motivation to work to achieve the goal? One must follow these simple steps:

- **Establish harmony within the team members**. It is not necessary that the members must think alike on everything. That would not be possible. They must be in agreement about the established goal and how to achieve it.

- **Everyone must appreciate the purpose of the goal**. They must know why it has to be attained.

- **Everyone must be aware of each other's responsibilities**. Without it there would be confusion.

- **Everyone must be aware of the timeframe**. A goal must be time-bound to be an ideal goal.

- **Everyone must be aware of reporting norms**. These must be established in the beginning. Without reporting one can easily slip or fail.

- **Be on the lookout for unexpected obstacles and problems**. There could be some miscalculations of facts, figures and time.

- **A good leader always has backup arrangements**. There will be the need to meet emergencies.

- **Appreciate and reward good work**. You will get better response the next time.

What should the leader do in the event of a failure to attain one's goal? It would be useful to follow these simple steps:

- **Do not blame any one person for the failure**. Share the blame with others.

83

- **Analyse the efforts that were made**. You must search for the cause of failure.
- **Learn from your failure**. It is not wrong to fail. It is wrong not to learn from failure.
- **Treat a failure as a temporary defeat**. This attitude will ensure an early success.

MOTIVATION AND INSPIRATION

An aspiring leader needs to understand the difference between motivation and inspiration. While motivation means to get a person interested in something, to inspire means to arouse an urge or ability to do something. While motivation is superficial and outward, inspiration touches a person deep within. It prepares a person for much greater things in life.

Inspiration awakens the angel within a person and puts him or her in contact with the most powerful source of energy – God! Irrespective of the faith and religion one follows, this happens when a person is deeply touched by an outstanding experience of faith. Once inspired a person is capable of doing great things. Some of the most outstanding artists, writers, performers and people in other leadership roles are known to have been inspired.

An aspiring leader cannot wait for inspiration, to get down to work. The person just needs to be self-motivated and fulfill responsibilities. Greater things will follow later.

POINTS TO PONDER

1. A leader is nothing without the support and cooperation of the people one works with.

2. In working with people, good etiquette and manners must be observed at all times.

3. Teams perform and achieve much more than individuals.

4. Delegation of responsibility is the key to increasing productivity.

5. To be useful, delegation must be effective.

6. The team members must be aware of the goals they are working to achieve.

7. Like the goals, the team members must also share the *Plan of Action*.

8. To ensure success, priorities must be assigned to the goals.

9. The leader must motivate the team members. Motivation helps arouse the interest of the team in the goals.

10. A variety of things motivate people. The leader must know and practise them.

11. Inspiration is a step ahead of motivation. It can help attain great things.

Step 5
Pitfalls to Avoid

Leadership is about people. It is common to see people asking a leader for favours or special considerations. This is something very natural to happen. However, this can affect the best of leaders in a negative way. It can make the leader feel superior in one way or another. This feeling of superiority can lead the person to several pitfalls and arrest the growth. In some situations it has even brought in degradation of thought and ruination.

A person is controlled by his or her thoughts. When the thoughts are positive they lead a person to wide-scale acceptance and recognition. When the thoughts are negative, one 'misleads' rather than lead. History has innumerable examples of negative leaders who snatched power, became dictators and led large groups and nations to ruin. These are exceptional cases and come to notice on rare occasions.

We are immediately concerned with the leadership roles individuals play in everyday life. A leader remains a leader as long as he or she performs. The moment a person fails to perform, people turn to another leader. This goes on throughout life. We see this happen everyday in the field of politics where roles change everyday. Leaders try new techniques.

The public seeks better leaders who can perform to their satisfaction. The leader then asks, "What went wrong? I am what I always was. Why did people turn away from me?" Little do such leaders realise that life is forever changing. Every little act is influencing life for better or worse. Unaware about them, leaders suffer pitfalls. Every upcoming leader would be at an advantage to know about these pitfalls. The knowledge would safeguard the leader from being let down.

COMPLACENCY

A common pitfall many leaders succumb to is complacency. To be complacent means to be satisfied with what one is doing. To be satisfied means that the person does not want to strive harder. When the leader is satisfied and does not want to exert harder, will the others put in their best effort? Certainly not! When the leader is satisfied, the feeling of complacency swiftly passes on to the team, and productivity suffers.

Beware of becoming complacent. John C. Maxwell warns, "Of all the things a leader should fear, complacency should head the list." Complacency ushers in decay, not growth. Life is dynamic. Change is a part of life. Either you grow or decay. It is an individual's choice as to which way one wants to go. Complacency only leads one towards decay. It may not happen suddenly. It will take its own time. By the time one discovers having suffered a pitfall, it is invariably too late to do anything about it. One must guard against it well ahead before an ugly situation emerges.

One of the most essential qualities in a leader is to be able to improve a little bit each day. If the person is already satisfied with what he or she is, or is achieving in everyday life, why would one want to improve oneself a little bit each day? The next obvious question is if a person is not willing to improve a little bit each day, can such an individual ever be recognised or acknowledged as a leader? If you want to be a leader in your field, do not give in to complacency. Ask yourself periodically, "Am I striving hard enough to grow, or am I slipping into complacency?" The choice is yours. Decide which way you want to go.

Think it over...

Man himself is the crowning wonder of creation; the study of his nature, the noblest study the world affords.

— *Gladstone*

IGNORING PEOPLE

If we are enjoying the fruits of development and progress through the many comforts we have in everyday life, it has been possible because of the great work our forefathers did in their respective fields. We stand tall because we stand on someone else's shoulder, benefiting from all that has been previously done. Just think about it. Are we grateful for all that we have received from our forefathers? The majority will agree that we are not. We find it difficult to give credit where it is really due. We live with the misconception that all that we enjoy is because of our own efforts.

Many young leaders fall an easy prey to this problem. They forget the people who have helped them at one time or another. This is true with relationships within the family, at the workplace, or even in the community where we live.

It feels good when a person helps us in a difficult moment, but once we are back into our 'comfort zone' we forget the favours extended to us. This can hurt the people who may have gone out of their way to be supportive, and are compelled to feel that the person 'uses' people to fulfil personal needs. Can a leader aspire confidence when he is labeled to 'use' people? Nothing hurts people more than being ignored.

An able leader moves forward with a smile, greeting people, shaking hands, exchanging pleasantries and looks directly into the eyes of the other, confirming a sincere relationship. The open attitude and enthusiasm convincingly arouse immediate confidence. The person feels wanted, and offers cooperation. What else would a leader desire? The next time you come across people who have at one occasion or another touched your life, do not ignore them. Extend a pleasant smile. Look into their eyes. Enquire how they are doing. Ask if you could be of any help to them. You will be remembered for your gesture.

FORGETTING NAMES

The best of leaders have on occasions been guilty of falling a prey to this pitfall. A person may fail to remember the name of an individual causing unnecessary hurt and ill will. It happens unintentionally, but is too vital to be ignored. To every person his or her name is the most pleasant sound to the ears. Whenever it is forgotten or wrongly pronounced people tend to take offence. It may be unintentional but anything that hurts individual sentiments pulls down the credibility of the person, and he or she fails to register as an able leader in everyday life.

People are not only offended when their names are forgotten or mispronounced, but equally so when their names are misspelled in letters and other communications. It happens too frequently. Some people speak out and complain; others tolerate it silently. Nonetheless people are very sensitive about their names. No leader can afford to ignore this sensitivity.

Looking at the situation from an aspiring leader's point of view, remembering names is not easy unless one meets frequently and has the opportunity to be using the name. Under these circumstances it is better for a person to confess one's weakness and ask the person to repeat the name so that it may not be mispronounced. This way one accepts human frailties, repeats the name to be heard clearly, and does not take offence. When writing letters and other communications it is good practice to check spellings, address, etc. That ensures freedom from taking offence.

LACK OF INTERACTION

With each passing day people are getting busy and involved in their own affairs. They appear to have no time for others. Therefore, there is a total lack of interaction amongst relatives, colleagues and friends. Some accept the situation and overlook it. A few are sensitive about this lack of interaction particularly from those they consider leaders or role models.

An able leader interacts with everyone he is connected with at home, at the workplace and in the society. This interaction may not be on a daily basis, but on special occasions like when one is sick, or there is a wedding or special occasion. Nobody invites people on the occasion of bereavement, but grief that is shared reduces immensely. People are grateful when others find time to be with them on these occasions.

Interaction with many people is a burden on one's time and effort. Leadership is all about sharing oneself with others when they need you. It would be wise to understand people's sensitivities and interact with them in time of need. When it is not possible to be present personally, a good leader makes up through a phone call, a personal communication or a visit at a suitable time. These activities may appear insignificant but they do enhance a leader's image in the minds of people.

ARE THEY FRIENDS OR ENEMIES?

A leader would obviously come across a variety of people. Many of them would be good, but a few may not be so. These few may have a negative outlook or their integrity may be doubtful. Such persons surround leaders particularly in the field of politics. One needs to be very careful about them because they could entice a person to drinking, drugs and activities of doubtful nature. They confess to being good friends but are really enemies in disguise. Unawares they are a challenge to every leader. One must be careful about them.

Steering through people of all kinds is difficult for any leader. However, this is part of a leader's role and one must go through it. One cannot afford to offend anyone. In matters pertaining to principles and integrity a leader needs to be firm and straightforward. Irrespective of what others may say or do one needs to be strict. On such occasions it is a person's character that matters. All great people have gone through such circumstances, and may have faced ridicule and undue criticism from so-called friends, but they faced the situation like a firm rock that cannot be moved. An able leader needs to use all the skills to be like that sometimes.

Beware of enemies disguised as friends. This is a nasty pitfall to become a prey to. Such people may appear harmless but they can let down a leader or make him or her dance to their tunes. Some would even blackmail. Nothing brings down a person faster than bad friends. Once again, the choice is yours. Which way do you want to go?

Think it over...

It is with certain good qualities as with the senses; those who have them not can neither appreciate nor comprehend them in others.

— *Rochefoucauld*

LACK OF APPRECIATION

One of the finest tools in the hand of every leader is the ability to appreciate one's colleagues who contribute personal effort to promote productivity or take one towards the goal in hand. Sometimes the leader fails to appreciate the effort or give credit where it is due, and the entire plan comes tumbling down like a house of cards.

It is a human weakness to be appreciated for whatever one contributes towards the success of an activity. The leader needs to be aware of the sensitivities of people. The leader must also know how to extend appreciation.

A variety of ways are used to express appreciation. In organisations, workers are given titles or positions to add to the prestige of a position. On special occasions prizes are awarded. Those who do not qualify for awards are presented 'Certificates of Appreciation' for participation and contributing to the success of the function. The photographs of outstanding performers are included in house journals or magazines. More than anything else, a word of praise, a pat on the back or a letter of appreciation does wonders to keep people motivated.

An able leader will need to be as careful about appreciating the efforts of those contributing towards success as one is about attaining a goal. One little lapse and everything can go flat. Appreciation is a time-tried effective tool. Every leader must use it to advantage.

INGRATITUDE

Just as lack of appreciation is resented, so is ingratitude. While one appreciates another for a special contribution or effort to take one towards the goal, ingratitude relates to being thankless for a special favour. Everyone needs each other's support, and when this support is extended, it is necessary that the person must be appropriately thanked for it. When the expression of gratitude is ignored there is obvious resentment and the leader suffers.

It is common for young leaders to rationalize the situation by saying that it was not because of the person's efforts that the work was done, but rather by the circumstances that changed the situation, or because of personal effort. This may be true. However, when a person is requested for a favour and the particular work is done, it is only right that some credit must be given to the person who extended the favour, and appropriate gratitude expressed in time. Even when it is not possible to meet personally to convey gratitude, it would be all right to express it through a small handwritten note or letter. This makes the person feel elated.

People who have the habit of saying "Thank you" for every little favour, however small it may be, are always admired and looked up to for their gracious behaviour. Goodwill gained through little gestures and courtesies go a long way in building up a good leader.

BEING RUDE AND SARCASTIC

Everyone has his or her strengths and weaknesses. A strange combination between the two contributes to build the personality. Leadership is synonymous with power over others. Using the power that comes from a particular position some leaders assert themselves by being rude and sarcastic. With a few it becomes a habit. Such people are often termed as "uppish". Many "bosses" are guilty of this indulgence.

Most people are not willing to accept rudeness or sarcasm. Even the subordinates feel that the person who leads them has no reason to use foul language. No one likes to be humiliated. It is an insult to their self-esteem. It is, therefore, not surprising that people avoid those who indulge in it.

Rude and sarcastic behaviour can be likened to use of brute force through speech. Just as people resist physical brute force, they also resist verbal brute force. No leader who aspires to rise further in life can afford to use such tactics to earn the respect of his co-workers. One cannot also expect them to put in their best efforts. Out of necessity some people may tolerate such behaviour. However, eventually it is the person who indulges in it who will suffer. All upcoming leaders need to be cautious about it.

Think it over...

Pride, like the magnet, constantly points to one object, self; but unlike the magnet, it has no attractive pole, but at all points repels.

— *Colton*

PRIDE

A good leader will find recognition. It is also natural to feel elated on being recognised. This elation leads a person to feeling proud. Appreciation and recognition are great motivating forces. Many leaders thrive upon them. As long as pride is within limits it continues to motivate people, but when it goes out of hand, people begin to resent it in a person. People are often heard saying, "He is too proud of his position to remember his old colleagues." This is the beginning of the unmaking of a leader. Should an aspiring leader risk it?

Pride is a deep pleasure or satisfaction gained from achievements, qualities or possessions. It also refers to self-respect. These are the positive aspects of the feeling of pride. Just across the borderline, pride also means an excessively high opinion of oneself. This is the negative aspect of the word. When a leader begins to hold an excessively high opinion of personal abilities, it is natural for the colleagues to resent it, particularly when they have contributed towards the attainment of a project. Everyone does understand that nothing can be achieved without the support and cooperation of others.

Aspiring leaders must understand that pride has both positive and negative aspects. While it is motivating to have pride as a positive force, it becomes destructive when accepted in the negative form. Bolingbroke simply explains, "Pride defeats its own end, by bringing the man who seeks esteem and reverence into contempt."

VANITY

Vanity is excessive pride in one's appearance or achievements. It also refers to the quality of being pointless or futile. Vanity is one step ahead of pride. It comes from the feeling that one has contributed more than others towards achieving a goal. No leader can afford to have such a feeling. The moment he or she indulges in it, the others begin to feel inferior and small, and it is not easy to accept a colleague or partner as superior. The leader immediately loses the respect of the colleagues.

Shakespeare simply asserts, "Vanity keeps persons in favour with themselves, who are out of favour with all others." Yet there is another aspect when Benjamin Franklin says, "Of all our infirmities, vanity is the dearest to us; a man will starve his other vices to keep that alive." Vanity emerges from self-love and one cannot totally avoid it. An aspiring leader needs to be careful that it does not come as a pitfall that restricts growth. While on one hand a leader is ruled by personal compulsions, on the other hand there is the need to carry along one's colleagues towards a goal.

ARROGANCE

A step ahead of pride and vanity is arrogance. A person becomes arrogant when he or she crosses the borderline between the positive and negative aspects of pride completely towards having too great a sense of one's own importance or abilities. This leads to self-destruction. History has innumerable examples of people who possessed many good qualities, but because of arrogance all was lost ultimately. World's best-known dictators met their end because of arrogance. One negative quality overshadowed all the leadership skills that they possessed.

Arrogance comes from over-confidence. Driven by passions rather than reason, over-confidence leads people to absurdities. Colleagues and subordinates never accept these kindly. In such situations the best of leaders lose their popularity. In extreme cases it leads to self-destruction.

To avoid the pitfall of arrogance every leader needs to be aware of the feeling of pride, which is the beginning of the road to arrogance. If pride is kept under control and used only as a motivating force, the leader grows. When pride leads to negative behaviour, it rapidly helps arrogance grow. No aspiring leader can afford to let this happen.

SHOWING RESENTMENT

When a member in a team fails to provide the necessary support and cooperation, a leader tends to fall prey to yet another pitfall in that he or she may show resentment about it. The leader feels that a point needs to be driven home; that this would get the person to act. However, it does not happen that way. The person concerned may have personal reasons for the way he or she has behaved. The person rationalizes the actions and counters the resentment by telling the leader that the fault is at the leader's end. This can lead to a small confrontation, and even something worse.

To avoid such situations a leader needs to follow-up on every team member to ensure that everyone is doing his or her bit. It is better to nip a problem in the bud rather than to let it grow into a major issue that affects the whole team. In circumstances where a person is not responsive, it would be advisable to seek the help of other team members, to distribute the responsibility to everyone. This way everyone knows what is going on, and there is no resentment at a later stage. In the event of a serious problem the team knows and appreciates the cause of the situation.

There will be situations where despite the care a leader may take a colleague may still not perform, and may let down the team. Under such circumstances rather than showing resentment, which is a natural thing to do, a leader must step ahead and ask the person if something is bothering him or her, and if it is necessary to provide some help. The person will appreciate the concern and will strive to put in greater effort the next time.

Allowing a feeling of resentment to linger is like not allowing a wound to heal. If you keep touching a wound, it will not heal. Left alone, it will heal without leaving a scar. When things go wrong a leader must ascertain all the facts of the situation before reacting to the situation.

ANGER

It is natural for a person to express anger in certain
circumstances. However, anger goes out of control very
easily. When angry a person uses language that is best
avoided, utters words that are best unspoken. The face
may flush, the heart palpitates, the blood pressure soars,
the mind becomes unsteady, and the limbs tremble. In
extreme cases the person may become violent. Anger,
just another emotion, when out of control may lead a
person to a situation it may be hard to get back from.

Anger is a strong feeling of extreme displeasure. The
cause of this displeasure could be a person or a situation.
Everyone desires a certain way of life, and when he or
she finds a situation that is not in harmony with what one
desires, there is frustration and cause for anger. It is natural
to give in to anger, but when out of control it no longer
remains an outlet for frustration, but rather becomes a
cause of serious concern.

An aspiring leader can easily become a prey to the
pitfalls of anger. A leader is likely to come across many
provocative situations because of several reasons, and if
one were to react to them without sufficient self-control it
would only end in futility. Self-control is necessary for the
positive use of anger. An aspiring leader needs to make

special effort to acquire this self-control. It is difficult, but not impossible.

JEALOUSY

To be jealous means to be envious of someone else's achievements or advantages. While it is all right to be protective of one's rights, privileges and possessions, the problem occurs when a person begins to compare trifling things with others. The famous poet and author, Cervantes, has rightly said, "Jealousy sees things always with magnifying glasses which make little things large, of dwarfs giants, of suspicions truths."

Jealousy is born out of self-doubt. A person may have all the facts, but jealousy misinterprets them, arouses suspicion and even self-destruction. To be jealous is to poison oneself. Can anything else be worse?

An aspiring leader cannot afford to be jealous of others. That would be suicidal, an end to the journey towards the goal. One should not compare oneself with others. Everyone is unique. Everyone is different. Everyone moves ahead in harmony with one's strengths and weaknesses. When everyone is different, would it be befitting to compare oneself with others? Everyone must accept oneself as a special person. Whenever in doubt one must strive to remove the cause of the doubt. One must work to get ahead with all of one's ability. When a person is constantly striving to improve oneself there is no cause for doubt or jealousy. One just gets ahead.

PROCRASTINATION

A very common pitfall that every aspiring leader needs to avoid is procrastination. In plain words, it means to delay, or postpone, an activity. It appears to be something that is harmless. Yet when a person habitually procrastinates, he or she may experience a sense of guilt. Procrastination is responsible for loss of productivity. Sometimes it may also be the cause for a crisis. It leads teammates and co-workers to feel that they have been let down. Occasionally procrastination could be accepted. However, when it becomes habitual it can have serious effects.

An aspiring leader cannot take procrastination lightly. If it happens too often the cause must be searched and examined. It could be due to psychological or physiological disorders. These may emerge from deep anxiety, lack of self-esteem, laziness or a self-defeating mentality. The physiological disorder could arise from the role of the prefrontal cortex causing poor organisation, loss of attention and procrastination. This could also be due to a condition described as *Attention Deficit Disorder*.

Every aspiring leader who has goals to attain and deadlines to be met must avoid procrastination at all costs. When things seem difficult and the going tough, a good leader does not put off the activities, but strives to do a little at a time, slowly moving towards the goal. A continued effort helps break the habit of procrastination, preparing the leader for greater responsibilities. A positive attitude is the best way to handle this common pitfall. With a high level of self-confidence one is always prepared for all kinds of situations.

Psychologists explain that persons who procrastinate could be the relaxed kind, who postpone the work in order to avoid stress. They find it comfortable to do work that is easy or fun to do. Then there is the tense type, who is unsure of their goals and is under pressure of time. Either way, procrastination gives the impression that a person is over-worked. This ultimately leads people to the problems of anxiety and stress. Setting goals and following correct time and work management techniques can help aspiring leaders to get over the habit of procrastination.

INDECISION

There is yet another pitfall that many aspiring leaders fall a prey to – indecision! In every leadership role it is necessary to take decisions. Taking a decision involves the responsibility of choosing between two or more options. With lack of confidence one is afraid of making a choice. The choice could be wrong. In such eventuality it could be embarrassing for the person making the choice. For obvious reasons most people prefer to avoid taking decisions. They pass on the "buck" either to the subordinates or the seniors, personally withdrawing to the comfort zone.

Taking decisions is an essential part of the leader's role. Not taking a decision is also a decision. It is a decision in favour of not taking a decision. It is a decision to leave this important responsibility to others. It is a decision to avoid responsibility. Can a leader be acknowledged or recognised under these circumstances? Certainly not! Such a person would immediately be labeled as incompetent, one who shuns responsibility. That would be the end of one's growth as a leader.

Never be afraid of taking a decision. Nobody can take all the right decisions all the time. Even the best of leaders are wrong sometimes. When no decision is taken the chances are that the situation will get worse. If a decision is taken after evaluating the facts and circumstances, generally the chances are that one would be sixty percent correct. That is much better than not taking any decision. When a person takes decisions regularly the chances are that they will be progressively better each time, increasing to seventy, eighty and even ninety percent correctness each time. That is what leadership is all about.

When a decision turns out to be wrong an aspiring leader should not try to rationalize it. One should also not pass the blame to the colleagues or subordinates. One must accept it with grace. In life, one always steps ahead with knowledge. It is the defeats and the failures that help shape knowledge into wisdom. To gain experience is to learn from one's mistakes. It is only the fool who never learns from mistakes. A good leader accepts the responsibility when things go wrong, and moves ahead. The ability to take the right decisions comes with practice, and this is possible only when a person acts in harmony with the circumstances and the situation.

Think it over...

Half of the secular unrest and dismal, profane sadness of modern society comes from the vain idea that every man is bound to be a critic of life.

— *Henry Van Dyke*

CRITICISM

Criticism is the simple expression of disapproval of an action. Nothing seems wrong with disapproval of something one does not like. However, criticism can be both positive and negative. When one sincerely expresses disapproval to make a person aware of a shortcoming, it should be welcome because it aims at improving the performance of the person. At the same time, one cannot ignore that two people may look at the same thing from two different angles and perspectives. What may appear as wrong to one may be right from the other's point of view. The aspiring leader needs to remember that he or she should avoid indulging in criticism. There are better ways of expressing concern and bringing the person to follow the correct direction.

Another way that a leader could be affected by the problem of criticism is when he or she is the target of criticism. The leader could have his or her reasons for the action. This could be discouraging to the leader, and could act as a major de-motivating force, arresting the progress towards the goal. In such an event the leader would do well to follow these simple steps:

- **Never let criticism provoke you**. Many an aspiring leader has resigned from important positions in response to provocation completely ending one's prospects of rising to higher positions of leadership.

- **Make a true assessment of the situation**. If one feels that he or she has made a mistake, this is the right time to make amends. Correct the fault. Follow up with greater determination.

- **Evaluate the critic's accusations**. If the leader is convinced that the action takes one towards the goal, accept criticism as an effort to derail your efforts to succeed. Just laugh it off. The solution lies in stepping up your efforts to move towards the goal.

POINTS TO PONDER

1. Even the most careful leaders need to avoid pitfalls.
2. Complacency is on the top of the list of common pitfalls leaders need to avoid.
3. It is people who make or break a leader. They should never be ignored.
4. A leader must remember names. One's name is the sweetest sounding word to everyone.
5. Lack of interaction makes people drift away from a leader.
6. A leader must be careful about enemies who come in the garb of friends and well-wishers.
7. Lack of appreciation will put off even the most committed workers.
8. Ingratitude is a sure way of offending people.
9. No leader can afford to be rude or sarcastic.
10. Excessive pride is the first step to a leader's decline.
11. Vanity is pride's companion. It does as much harm to a leader.
12. Arrogance is a step ahead of pride. No one likes arrogance in a leader.
13. A person's failure to support the leader should not be responded with show of resentment.

14. When angry a leader must maintain self-restraint.
15. Jealousy magnifies problems. It must be avoided at all times.
16. Procrastination leads a person towards failure.
17. Indecision can rob a leader of success and reputation.
18. All criticism must be evaluated from a positive point of view.

Step 6
Developing Leadership Qualities

We have earlier observed that there is a leader within each person. Everyone is blessed with an opportunity to serve in small roles as a leader in the home and at the workplace. The majority takes these opportunities in their stride. They do not take them as opportunities for personal development or growth. Only a few make special efforts to grow as leaders in different spheres of life.

It has been repeatedly said that leaders are not born. Leaders develop by acquiring special skills and abilities. We have already discussed how leadership opportunities come our way in everyday life. We have also seen how these opportunities offer new dimensions in our personal lives, and can take us to great heights in the service of mankind and personal growth. We are also aware of what abilities contribute to make a good leader.

While many skills and abilities of good leaders have been discussed, one must understand that it is not possible to acquire all of them. Every person is unique. Everyone works in harmony with one's temperament. Different people acquire a variety of skills and abilities. They choose abilities that would benefit them. It is an individual choice and one cannot comment upon it. Leaders are required in every field of activity. Each finds a position in an area of one's choice.

Depending upon one's strengths a person adopts and develops special skills. However, there are some qualities that are common to all leaders. For example, all leaders need to be confident and committed. They need to be honest and determined. They must possess good communication skills. There are several other skills and abilities that would interest aspiring leaders. Let us see how one can transform oneself to become an acknowledged leader in his or her field of activity.

THE NEED FOR CHANGE

One cannot transform oneself into a leader without a willingness to change for the better. One progresses by trying new activities and making them work. The vast majority resists change. They would prefer that the circumstances and the people around them should change. Every person lives in a comfort zone and resists getting out of it. Even when motivated to step out of the comfort zone and experience the great potential that is waiting to be tapped, one is only temporarily stirred to action. One soon falls back into the comfort zone, rationalizing one's actions.

It is not difficult to understand this attitude. Hidden within change is an element of uncertainty. From this uncertainty a variety of fears emerge. These fears keep people away from change. People are afraid to lose what they have in lieu of what they anticipate in uncertainty. To face fear one needs to act boldly to face new circumstances. Greater things are not too far away.

People also resist change because they do not possess the knowledge to step ahead with confidence. They do not know how to change the circumstances around them. They wonder if the change would take away whatever they are enjoying presently. They are uncertain whether the change would take them towards progress and development. The aspiring leader needs to know what he or she would like to attain. They need to be aware of the circumstances. They need to acquire knowledge to face the new situations.

TAKE CONTROL OF YOURSELF

Before a person can develop leadership skills and abilities, it is necessary that one must take complete control over oneself. Most people have the bad habit of blaming other people and situations for their failure. These people blame everyone and everything for their failure to succeed. They never accept that they are responsible for both success and failure.

Take a look at what you are doing today. Is everything not aimed at making things better for tomorrow, and the day after? Are we not working for a better future? We are doing it today, and we will do it again tomorrow. In the same way, we worked yesterday, the day before and even years earlier. We are today what we worked for yesterday. If we lack contentment, let us not look for reasons elsewhere, but within ourselves. A mature person accepts responsibility for everything pertaining to him or her. One should not hesitate to accept the situation when things go wrong. One should be willing to make amends. One should be ready for change. One should be ready to get ahead in life.

Do not overlook that you are a unique person. A vast majority of people is not what they want to be. Each person projects several images. People see and accept them in different forms. The situation becomes worse because people are not in harmony with the self. The cause is easy to understand. Everyone is trying to condition the other in harmony with one's thoughts and perception. The parents, the teachers, friends and others are busy trying to condition each other all the time. You could be as guilty of doing the same to others. The process of conditioning leads people to make comparisons amongst each other. This only creates confusion and mental restlessness. It makes people feel inferior. To avoid unpleasantness people try to conform to each other. One finds only temporary happiness by such conformity to others.

Take control and be yourself. You are unique. Accept this fact and do not try to be what you are not. Do not let anyone compel you to do anything you do not like. This is your life. Live, as you would like to. Do it your way. You are aspiring to be a leader in your field. Let nothing hold you back. You are the master of your own life.

Think it over...

The shortest and surest way to live with honour in the world is to be in reality what we would appear to be; all human virtues increase and strengthen themselves by the practice and experience of them.

— *Socrates*

BECOME VIRTUOUS

An essential quality one desires in every leader is reliability. One should be able to unhesitatingly trust a leader. The basis of trust would always be the person's ability to handle and fulfil responsibility. To assess this ability one would look at a person as one composite being with many abilities that together reflect the person's character. This, in turn, comes from many seemingly insignificant experiences that over a period contribute to the building of character. Goodness comes from being virtuous.

One derives great strength from being virtuous. A virtuous person is recognised, acknowledged and respected everywhere. Some of the common virtues that help build character are patience, tolerance, politeness, courtesy, friendliness, sincerity, truthfulness, honesty, moderation, flexibility, forgiveness, generosity, thoughtfulness, love, benevolence, being charitable, purity, persistence and several others.

With the development of virtues the positive influences within a person develop, and he or she is able to generate positive vibrations that not only influence the person, but also those one comes in contact with. In practical terms, love of people leads one to respect, being gentle, cooperative, generous and benevolent. In the same way happiness leads to laughter, cheerfulness and being carefree. Peace is expressed as patience, tolerance, sincerity and silence. Of all virtues, humility is most important to the leader because it does not let the feeling of self-importance take over. It is through humility that a person can experience divine radiance, peace and inner happiness. Humility raises ordinary people to angelic heights. With these qualities a leader can achieve much.

All aspiring leaders want to know how they can develop these virtues in their everyday life. It is simple.

Practice these virtues everyday. In school every child is repeatedly reminded that one must be truthful, honest and thoughtful of others. However, since this teaching does not form a part of the curriculum one does not give it the importance it deserves. One only remembers what is ingrained in the mind by the parents through little suggestions in childhood. These become evident in adult life.

To become virtuous, a person must first write down all the virtues that one would like to adopt as a part of self-development. Once this list is ready, choose one virtue that you would opt for every morning. Make a deliberate effort to practise it at home, at the workplace and in the society throughout the day. In the evening review how you have fared. Where did you fail? Why? When you become conscious of the need for the virtue, it begins to get ingrained in the mind. The next day, you could try to practise yet another virtue. This way, in a week, you would have practised seven virtues. Repeat them over the next week, and the week thereafter until you feel they are a part of you. You will begin to experience a definite change within you, as these virtues become a part of you.

To gradually develop yourself follow these simple suggestions:

- Lead a simple life that others can emulate. Eat and dress simply.
- Always look at life from the others' point of view. This will generate thoughtfulness for others in thought, word and deed. Accept people as they are, and not as you would want them to be.
- Think positive. Be optimistic. If negative thoughts enter the mind, replace them with positive thoughts.

Replace hatred with love, and sorrow with joy. It is better to forgive rather than take revenge.

- As a God's child, one should act like Him. He has blessed you with patience, tolerance, love, mercy and compassion. Let the angel within guide you.
- Practice silence. This helps to conserve mental and physical energy, observe serenity and increase concentration.

DEVELOP SELF-CONFIDENCE

The first step to becoming a leader is to develop self-confidence. It enhances one's self-esteem. Millions of capable persons fail to become leaders because they lack self-confidence. They enjoy low self-esteem. This could be due to their negative thoughts about their appearance, the family background or may be because they cannot forget an unpleasant past. To develop self-confidence one must overcome these trivial thoughts. Through control of one's thoughts, feelings and actions one can develop new habits and self-confidence.

To develop confidence, evaluate your abilities periodically. Review your successes and failures. Your past performances can always be improved upon. You need to take a new look at your personality. Devote more time on activities where you have achieved success. Acquire knowledge that can help you achieve still greater success. Try a hand at new activities. Success in a variety of activities is the best confidence builder. Keep repeating your successes. Never doubt your abilities. Develop new interests. Read books on new subjects. Join a club. Learn to sing, or play a musical instrument. Go out where you can meet new people. Your confidence will grow.

THINK POSITIVE

The leader's success depends upon how he or she thinks. Thoughts are the basis of a personality. Leadership skills and abilities are dependent upon good thoughts. One must remember that all thoughts are important. The thoughts can be positive or negative. Both require the same kind of effort. However, the results are different. Positive thoughts release positive energy and negative thoughts release negative energy.

Very few people provide good thoughts. Since they are scarce, people accept them with some doubt and hesitation. Good thoughts are deep-rooted and backed by determination. They cannot be easily destroyed. They flourish in the company of good people.

Bad thoughts are available in abundance. They are easily accepted and freely propagated. When bad thoughts are avoided, evil and sin reduce proportionately. Such is the influence of thoughts.

A leader must understand that while the personality is shaped with thoughts, a leader also persuades others through thoughts. When good thoughts are planted, the fruit from them is bound to be good. The dynamics of good thoughts inspires everyone to be good and do well.

Think it over...

We must truly serve those whom we appear to command; we must bear with their imperfections, correct them with gentleness and patience, and lead them in the way to heaven.

— *Fénelon*

DEAL WITH PEOPLE KINDLY

In any leadership role one needs to deal with people. They are the chief concern of every leader. When it is possible to handle them well the productivity increases; there is much to attain. This subject has already been discussed earlier. However, when developing leadership skills and abilities this subject needs special attention. No amount of emphasis is enough. Here are a few observations and guidelines about relationships that every leader can learn from and use in everyday life:

- Everyone deserves respect. We need to appreciate that everyone is different, is right from his or her point of view, and it is natural for people to be sensitive to certain things.

- The usual courtesies must be extended to everyone. Every person is an individual in his or her own right. People respond with goodwill provided one takes interest in their welfare.

- People must know that you care for their feelings. Extend simple courtesies like saying "thank you", "excuse me", "I beg your pardon" or "I'm sorry" in everyday life.

- Look at people from their point of view. Everyone considers himself or herself important. His or her name is the sweetest word they like to hear. To them personal emotions and feelings are very important. These must be respected.

- Everyone has a personal philosophy about life. One will insist that it is the best way to live. Accept it as a part of the person.

- Only one out of every twenty people looks at life from a positive viewpoint. Negative thoughts and feelings predominate in the lives of the other nineteen.

- Fears of all kinds dominate the lives of the vast majority of people. They are afraid of criticism, of being ridiculed, of losing health, a loved one, or money, of failing in life, or death, and a whole lot of other things.

- People will disagree that they have failed because they are negatively oriented. They will blame their failures on other people and situations.

- People respect those who remember their names, appreciate them sincerely, listen to what they say and respect their hopes and aspirations.

- The way you speak helps persuade people. Speak in their language. Speak simply. When you act and speak in a superior way people are made to feel ignorant and inferior.

- People are generally interested in many things. Speak their language and share similar interests. A person with many interests finds it easy to converse with others.

- Do not indulge in gossip. It has never done anybody any good.

- Do not criticize people. Negative criticism is harmful. It repels people. Before sitting on judgment visualize how you would have acted if you were in the other person's position.

- Do not get into an argument. It has never helped win friends. You may win the argument but will lose the friend.

- Do not give opinion or advice unless it is asked for. An opinion is just a suggestion. Leave the acceptance of your suggestion to the choice of the other person.
- Do not be concerned about others more than what is necessary.
- Do not be selfish or insincere. The other person will see through it easily. Nobody appreciates insincerity and selfishness.
- Do not speak or act in a manner that your honour or integrity would be doubted. When defamatory facts about others come to your knowledge, just bury them.
- Keep your problems to yourself. People seek help from those who are self-sufficient, not from those who are in trouble.
- Radiate a positive atmosphere, not one of problems and gloom. People avoid those who brood and sulk.
- Smile. People will smile back at you. Laugh. People will laugh with you.
- Optimism and enthusiasm are contagious. They help attract friends.
- Accept good time management as a part of daily life. Let people know that you care for their time.
- Compliment others for their achievements and success. Praise and appreciation help win the toughest of people. People like you when you like them.
- There are no shortcuts to winning and influencing people.

- To win people over on a long-term basis there is no substitute for sincerity, integrity and honourable conduct.
- Virtues like truthfulness, honesty and a noble character are recognised only over a long period of time.
- Relationships built upon a strong foundation are satisfying and lasting.
- When one enjoys the goodwill of people, it is the finest form of power that anyone can possess. Used for the benefit of others, it grows. When used for self-appeasement it diminishes.
- Self-sufficiency is a great power-builder. All people look up to those who are so blessed.
- Do not insist that people should change. If it is necessary, use tact and patience. Identify areas where you and the person agree. When both are in agreement, tactfully suggest the benefits of the proposed change.
- It is an uphill task to change others. If a person were to accept them as they are, and not as one would want them to be, the world would become a more agreeable and happy place to live in.
- People accept to change when they realise that a changed attitude towards life would bring them success and happiness.
- Making a change becomes easy when a person identifies better ways to fulfil personal desires.
- Success stories motivate people to change. Touching a person emotionally also encourages one to change.

- People are not receptive to new ideas all the time. Individual receptivity is governed by biorhythms. Therefore, suggestions for a change must be synchronized with a period of high receptivity. This makes it easier to attain one's purpose.
- Make success your companion. Your success will motivate others. People follow those who score goals in life.
- Do not go overboard with pleasing people. Nobody has ever succeeded in pleasing everyone.
- Personal happiness should not be sacrificed in making others happy. Live a balanced life that has a place for friends and companions. Be with people to enjoy the relationship, yet stay aloof to enjoy privacy.

Think it over...

Suit the action to the word, the word to the action; with this special observance, that you overstep not the modesty of nature.

— *Shakespeare*

COMMUNICATION SKILLS

For a leader it is not sufficient to be knowledgeable, experienced and wise. If one is unable to communicate effectively with others, one cannot lead effectively. It is essential to communicate effectively to lead well.

To be able to communicate means to be able to impart or exchange thoughts, opinion and information. It also refers to something imparted, interchanged or

119

transmitted. Generally, it refers to the use of speech or writing, as is done through verbal or written messages from person to person.

The sheer presence of people at a place helps communicate feelings and emotions. We see it happening every day. The feelings and emotions can be both positive and negative. Very often intimate thoughts and feelings are shared even without uttering a word. Much is communicated even through silence. People use it as a tool to introspect, or go deep within in search of one's true self. Silence is also a tool to punish others when one refuses to talk to express resentment. One sees this frequently amongst couples, or children and parents. Sometimes, the friends stop speaking to express hurt feelings.

The way one conducts oneself, speaks or dresses also communicates an image of a person. Many go out of the way to look smart, charming and beautiful by the way they dress or use makeup. The fragrances men and women use also convey a message. In a temple, a mosque, a church or any other place of prayer people not only pray or pay obeisance to a deity, but communicate with each other through positive vibrations that are a source of great pleasure and peace.

The aspiring leader would do well to understand and follow these simple rules about written communication:

- Use a language that others can understand. It is all right for highly educated people to use high-flown language. It is useless to the common man.
- Do not use abbreviations or words and phrases used by specific professionals and experts. The common reader does not understand them.

- Use words that are easy to understand. When choosing between two words, use one that is common.
- When writing, keep to the point. Most people tend to deviate.
- Let the matter to be conveyed progress logically.
- Write as few words as possible. After you have completed writing, revise the text to condense it. Keep the essentials and trim the frills.
- Do not write what the reader already knows.
- Avoid unnecessary phrases. Use simple words.
- Write with a positive outlook. Always avoid the negative.
- When you have written what you wanted to, just stop. Revise the text.

To ensure that the communication is effective, the aspiring leader will do well to remember the 5 Cs. The communication must be:

- **Clear**: It must tell clearly what is to be done.
- **Concise**: If the communication is lengthy the message may be lost in the words.
- **Courteous**: It has been observed that requests promote action sooner than an order.
- **Convincing**: Unless the reader is convinced that the request needs to be acted upon, the communication will not be acted upon.
- **Complete**: If the communication leaves behind an element of doubt, it will not be complete. Action will not be forthcoming.

There is another straightforward way of promoting effectiveness in a written message. The message should not only specify who should perform the desired action, but also:

- What is to be done?
- Why it is to be done?
- How it is to be done?
- When it is to be done?
- Where it is to be done?

There is another school of thought, which suggests that to make a communication effective, one must remember the ABC of writing.

A is for **attention**. The communication must immediately attract the attention of the reader. Unless the reader is attentive no action can be expected.

B is for **brevity**. The message must be as brief as possible. It is easy to get lost amongst words if the message is lengthy.

C is for **convincing**. Unless the reader is convinced of the need for action, the message will fail to be effective.

When a communication conveys all that needs to be said, and there are no doubts in the mind of the reader, it is an effective communication. It will get the reader to act.

SPEAKING SKILLS

Speaking skills are closely linked with leadership skills. Leaders who possess good speaking skills are able to influence and persuade people easily. It is for this ability that many a leader is acknowledged and recognised immediately. Those who do not possess this ability need to depend upon other skills for attaining their goal. That takes much longer. Leaders like Swami Vivekanand are known to have swayed opinion when addressing the International Convention of Religions in Chicago. History reveals how leaders have charged the feelings and emotions of people to bring about marked changes. Eminent personalities like Mahatma Gandhi and Mother Teresa were not orators, but stood high above others as leaders. They spoke the language of the common man. People looked forward to hear them.

Good public speaking skills are an asset to every leader. However, leaders lead by example, not only by speech. A speaker is more effective when he or she possesses leadership abilities. Speaking skills and leadership qualities go hand in hand. When a group of people have to be persuaded they must be convinced that the leader has put into practice what he wants them to do. People are always willing to follow an accepted leader. Even if the speaker is new to the audience but his credentials highlight leadership characteristics, the audience will find it easier to accept him and his suggestions.

An aspiring leader is never content to learn only the basics of public speaking. He needs to know and practice much more to become a model person who can inspire and motivate others by the example of personal life. Just as one grows as a leader, one can use speaking skills with greater authority.

Here are a few tips for an effective presentation:
- **Be relaxed**. You speak better when you are re-laxed.

- **Breathe deeply**. The additional oxygen adds to your confidence.
- **Be prepared**. Good preparation promotes self-confidence.
- **Practice before you make a presentation**. That helps perfect the presentation.
- **Believe in what you are going to speak**. There is a connection between what you feel and what you speak.
- **Speak naturally** as you would to friends.

Think it over...

A day once gone will never return. Therefore, one should be diligent each moment to do good. We reach the goal of good life by pious work.

— *Mahavir*

TIME MANAGEMENT

Time is a valuable gift God has granted everyone. It flows like a perennial river. It flows from the past and recedes into the future. Every individual has been given a limited number of years, months and days to experience it. Since it is a limited commodity, and once lost it cannot be redeemed, the proper utilisation of time is a matter of concern to all leaders. Time is a capital, not an income. No one can have more or less of it. Like any capital, it is precious. It must be put to the best use. This capital should initially be used to acquire personal skills and abilities, and later be used to be effective at home, at the workplace and in the society.

An efficient person may not necessarily be a good time manager. One could be efficient, and yet not be effective. Good time management emphasizes effectiveness, and not efficiency. To be efficient, one needs to **do things right.** To be effective means to **do right things**. Time management is all about setting the right goals, choosing the right priorities and acting upon them. Here are a few common observations about time management:

- Nobody is born a good time manager. The only way to becoming one is to learn about it.
- There are no shortcuts. One has to learn it just as one would learn any other skill.
- It cannot be learnt overnight. It will require persistent effort over a long time.
- People who come from disciplined families, or have studied in schools where great importance is given to discipline, learn faster.
- Those who insist that they do not need time management techniques are really closing their eyes to reality. They are building walls around them. This way they will fail to take advantage of time.
- When a person decides to become a good time manager, it is a lifetime commitment to becoming an effective person.
- Good time management begins with an understanding of oneself, with personal motivation, and by being aware that it will promote greater productivity and personal fulfilment.

THE BIORHYTHM PATTERN

The biorhythm pattern refers to a recurring cycle in the functioning of an organism, such as the daily cycle of keeping awake and sleeping. Each day we experience a day and a night. We also experience the changes in weather and climate affecting human beings, plants and animal life. Biorhythms reflect rhythmic changes, caused by hormones, affecting the physical state and activity patterns of plants and animals. The seasonal changes cause hibernation and influence breeding and migratory patterns in animals, and flowering in a variety of plants. The hormonal changes are caused by the variation in the length of the day. These changes communicate the time of the year to the plants and animals.

The circadian rhythm affecting the metabolic rhythm is based on the changes in the 24-hour day, and is found in most living beings. The sleeping and waking patterns depend upon it. The body temperature and the moods also follow a set rhythm. In sick people, the body temperature, blood pressure and the pulse are recorded at fixed times each day to observe these changes. These changes become obvious when a person travels swiftly in a jet plane into areas with different timings, and sleeping and waking patterns. The biological changes are described as 'jet lag', and it takes some time before the body gets adjusted to the new environments and timings.

The variations in the biorhythms affecting human beings are based on the changes in the 24-hour day. These affect the body temperature, blood pressure, the level of energy, attentiveness, appetite, sleeping and waking patterns and a whole lot of activities. The moods also follow a set rhythm. The heart too beats to a rhythm.

The menstrual cycle in women, and the sex drive in both men and women are also controlled by these rhythms. These can be traced to the activities of the hypothalamus and the pituitary glands. The hormones secreted by these glands are responsible for these variations. Unfortunately, the details are still not fully understood.

An individual's body temperature is lowest between 4.00 and 6.00 a.m. It increases gradually by mid-morning, and one experiences a higher level of energy. Those who sleep late and also rise late experience increase in energy levels later in afternoon. Since biorhythms vary in different people one must personally assess levels of energy at different times of the day. Efficiency varies with the biorhythms. Taking advantage of this fact, the more difficult and challenging assignments can be handled when the efficiency is at a peak, and the routine jobs can be handled at other times. This ensures high productivity and better utilization of time. Understanding biorhythms can help a leader to perform effectively.

Think it over...

I would like to amend the idea of being in the right place at the right time. There are many people who were in the right place at the right time but didn't know it. You have to recognize when the right place and the right time fuse and take advantage of that opportunity. There are plenty of opportunities out there. You can't sit back and wait.

— *Ellen Metcalf*

WORKING TO PRIORITIES

To be effective as a leader one must work on the basis of priorities. Generally, these are classified as urgent, important and routine. However, it is not easy to understand how to place an activity in each of the three classifications. Aspiring leaders also like to know if the activities can be described only as urgent, important and routine, or could there be other combinations?

An activity is best described as very important when the attainment of the goal depends directly upon it. It would be important if the attainment of the goal depends upon it indirectly. It would be less important if it contributes only to enhance the quality of the goal. It is unimportant if does not affect the goal.

Urgency describes the relationship between the activity and time. It would be very urgent if time were a critical factor. For example, a tax return has to be filed before a fixed date. The activity would be urgent when time is a crucial factor to complete the activity. When the activity is essential but the period to complete the activity can be extended, it would be described as less urgent. If the time factor does not affect the goal, then it is not urgent.

The next step is to decide upon the priorities. Give top priority to whatever is both important and urgent. The second should be to whatever is important. The third position must go to whatever is urgent, and finally the fourth position goes to whatever has lower importance and urgency. This task may appear difficult to begin with, but with practice one soon becomes perfect in prioritizing activities.

You could follow these simple steps to prioritize activities:

1. Prepare a list of all the activities that need to be done.
2. Mark each activity as A1, A2, A3 and A4 depending upon the importance of the activity in attaining the goal.
3. Mark each activity as B1, B2, B3 and B4 depending upon the urgency in attaining the goal.
4. On the basis of the markings make a fresh list according to priorities assigned to the activities.
5. If some of the activities can be delegated to others, do the needful.
6. Of the remaining activities personally follow up on activities of top importance.

You will soon be attaining much more than what you have been doing earlier.

POINTS TO PONDER

1. Leaders develop by acquiring skills and abilities.
2. Change is an essential part of learning. A leader must accept it as an element for growth and development.
3. A mature person accepts responsibilities for both successes and failures.
4. Accepting a virtuous life is a sure way to personal development.
5. To develop confidence one must devote more time on activities where success has been achieved.

6. Leadership skills and abilities become meaning-ful with good thoughts.
7. To maintain good relationships one must deal with people kindly.
8. A leader must regularly upgrade his or her com-munication skills.
9. Good speaking skills help promote one as a leader.
10. A good leader must manage time effectively.
11. A leader must recognise one's biorhythm pattern. It helps personal effectiveness.
12. A good leader promotes productivity by working on the basis of priorities.

Step 7
Becoming an Effective Leader

It is not sufficient to be a leader. Everyone has the leader in him or her, and will get the opportunity to put the skills to use. To be acknowledged and recognised it is important that one should be an effective leader, one who makes things happen. It is helpful to know the basics of leadership, the elements that contribute to the making of a leader, and also the pitfalls to avoid. It would also be useful to learn the intricacies of building good relationships. However, to be an effective leader, it takes a little more.

One needs to be a good person. One must be attractive to draw others' attention. One needs to be confident of oneself and one's abilities. One must have a positive attitude towards life. One must have a vision, and work on the basis of long-term and short-term goals. One must be able to communicate well, and to speak well in public. One must be able to sell oneself to others. With all this, there is still need for a little more. To be an effective leader one must possess a few more skills and abilities. Let us consider some of them.

A SELF-STARTER

Have you observed how on the press of a button some motorbikes start? Others start with a kick. Both may be new and well tuned. The difference is in the self-starter. It helps start the motor on the press of a button. The difference between a leader and an effective leader is the way one gets going. While one may need to be kick started, the other is a self-starter. The effective leader gets into action the moment something needs to be done.

To be a self-starter one needs to be self-motivated. One cannot motivate others unless one is personally motivated. At home when a person is enthusiastic, the spouse soon becomes enthusiastic also. The children follow thereafter. This is exactly what happens when a leader sets out to achieve something. The effective leader is enthusiastic, and soon passes this enthusiasm to others in the team.

What makes a leader a self-starter? Every person is unique. Every person is sensitive to different kinds of things. It is not possible to generalize how a person would react to a certain stimulus. However, when people know themselves well and can recognise their biorhythms that stimulate them more at some times and a little less at other times, they can ride on the waves effortlessly, doing the more difficult tasks during peak periods and routine jobs during lean periods. It has been observed that when the rhythms peak one is most efficient. Ideas flow easily. One feels fit and enthusiastic. One is ready for the most difficult assignments. It is often said that the person is 'inspired'. The inspiration flows from deep within making the person very effective.

The next obvious thing that the aspiring leader wants to know is: Can a leader wait for inspiration to come? Would that not affect the timeframe of a particular job at hand? No, a leader with a task to do cannot wait. Yes, if one were to wait for inspiration, it would not be possible to maintain the timeframe. The important thing to understand is that some of the most remarkable things have been achieved when the biorhythms peaked. While these rhythms vary seasonally, they also function on a day-to-day pattern, making a person more effective at some time of the day. One can take advantage of this fact.

It has also been observed that individuals respond to certain external influences that generate enthusiasm within them. These influences stimulate greater productivity. Appreciation and praise are great stimulants. They motivate a person immediately. However, the effective leader can use these on the teammates only. How can one attract appreciation and praise? Surely the leader cannot depend upon this stimulus. As an alternative, the leader can feed the mind with thoughts of appreciation and praise that awaits him or her on the completion of the assignment. These thoughts can be as stimulating as actual appreciation and praise. Effective leaders use their thought processes to gain personal benefit.

Amongst other things that are known to influence people towards productive activity are music, the company of nature, flowers, the presence of friends or loved ones. It has been observed that each time people respond to a particular influence in the same way. This explains why people find a walk in the park stimulating, or feel charged to work after a short holiday over the weekend. People go to hill stations and places near rivers, lakes or the sea because this puts them in touch with nature. This also explains why people like to hear different kinds of music. One can also appreciate why people are attracted towards particular individuals, and not others in general.

It is for a person to find out what stimulates one more than the other. All effective leaders have their own stimulants and use them to tune their mind and abilities to be productive. The aspiring leader must understand that to be effective it is necessary to be a self-starter. It is the effective leader who must set the ball rolling. If the leader is hesitant, why should someone else do it?

Think it over...

Be such a man, and live such a life, that if every man were such as you, and every life a life like yours, this earth would be God's Paradise.

— *Phillips Brooks*

THE UNENDING INSPIRATION

While still on the subject of different stimuli that influence individuals to be motivated and inspired to perform better, the greatest source of unending motivation and inspiration can be found in God. It is immaterial what faith or religion one adopts or follows, but this unending source of energy and power is available to everyone irrespective of one's faith, caste, colour or creed. Millions of people draw upon this source every day. It gives them strength to move on.

The temples, mosques, gurudwaras and churches and other places of prayer are full of people in search of power that one derives from God. It does not matter in what shape or form your faith guides you to see God. There is one God. Only people see Him in different forms. He fits into all of them because He has no form. He is a spot of light that energizes the whole universe, pervading into every being and thing. He resides within each of us. We cannot see or feel Him because of our own negative activities. Just as layers of dust covering a mirror render it unfit to see our image, our negative activities keep us away from the God within us. Virtuous people can feel God within them. They can talk to Him through prayer. He responds to them through their conscience.

It is difficult to explain but some of the most difficult problems are solved through prayer. People wonder how is it possible for God to respond to millions of prayers simultaneously. It may be difficult for individuals to respond to the requests from more than a few people, but for God it is possible. A little part of Him is there within each of us, and this keeps the connection alive. The moment God decides to withdraw, the individual is declared dead. The remains are consigned to the dust.

Prayers may be said with or without rituals. The rituals only help in focusing your mind towards God. The real thing is your desire to connect with God. Speak in a language that you would use with a friend or a loved one. Thank Him for whatever He has blessed you with. Ask Him to guide you. Ask Him to give you strength, patience, and tolerance and to help you become virtuous in everyday life. Soon you will begin to experience a new power within you. This will add to your personality, and help guide you to lead the way in whatever you take up.

THE CHALLENGE OF CHANGE

The biggest problem before every leader is the challenge of change. If one were to keep doing whatever one has always been doing, the results would be what they have always been. If no improvement is desired there would be no need for leaders. The simple thing would be to keep doing what you are doing. But there would neither be growth nor any improvement.

When development is desired, and a person is assigned the responsibility to bring it about, the first thing that comes to mind is what should be immediately changed to bring about growth and development. Both of these need a changed outlook, a different way of working. We have already seen earlier that people resist change. They are afraid what the changed circumstances hold in store for them. Would it be for better or worst? This resistance is a great challenge to every leader. Those who cross this hurdle succeed.

Everyone is different. Everyone looks at the same situation differently. With all of one's motivational skills it becomes difficult for leaders to break the resistance. The fault lies in the leaders desiring people to change the way they think. How can any leader say that his or her way of thinking is best? Is the leader willing to assure success? Would the leader agree to compensate others in the event of a failure? Of course not! Then why should the leader insist upon his or her way of thinking to be the best?

The solution does not lie in the leader changing the mindset of the team members, but in jointly agreeing to adopt a common goal, and working to attain it. The emphasis should not be on change, but on agreement. No team ever agrees to live similar kinds of life. They only agree to adopt a goal because there is something in it for them. The goal fulfils some tangible or intangible needs, and there is no fear that is a part of change. Once the goal is agreed upon, it becomes easy to accept a joint plan to attain it. It becomes still easier if the team members are involved in the planning stage. Except in special circumstances, if the members also agree on the division of responsibilities and fixing deadlines the leader's work becomes still easier. The leader can then direct and follow up the progress to ensure success.

When a change is definitely necessary, the leader needs to set examples through his or her own activities and lifestyle. Without that it would be sheer hypocrisy to preach one thing and follow quite another. At all times the leader needs to protect and respect the dignity of labour, and should never consider any work too small or petty. All leaders are tested from time to time, and only those who pass are accepted and recognized as leaders.

Think it over...

Learning, if rightly applied, makes a young man thinking, attentive, industrious, confident, and wary; and an old man cheerful and useful. It is an ornament in prosperity, a refuge in adversity, an entertainment at all times; it cheers in solitude, and gives moderation and wisdom in all circumstances.

— Palmer

USE YOUR STRENGTHS TO SUCCEED

The life of every person is ruled by two distinct factors – the strengths and the weaknesses. While the strengths add on to one's confidence and the ability to get ahead, the weaknesses act as obstacles. A leader's life is no different. To be effective, a leader needs to give special emphasis to one's strengths. Simultaneously, one must also make an effort to get over the weaknesses.

To emphasize upon one's strengths means to become more virtuous and use skills and abilities that are well developed in a person. There are many kinds of skills and abilities that contribute to one's success at home, the workplace and the community. Some get along well with people, have good communication and speaking skills or are as comfortable away from home, as they are at home. Others may have an analytical outlook or be great with accounts and figures. Some others may be kind, caring and sympathetic.

Each of these would obviously be capable of leading only in fields where these abilities can be used. When a person tries to get into an activity without the necessary abilities, it would only invite failure. This explains why two out of every five persons are doing the wrong kind of jobs. They are unhappy with what they are doing. This invites mediocrity, and not success. A good leader cannot afford to act this way. One must work in a field where one can put the strengths to the best use at home, at the workplace and in the society.

ELIMINATE THE WEAKNESSES

Just as it is necessary to use one's strengths to succeed, it is equally important to eliminate one's weaknesses. These may be holding a person from success. Some of the very common weaknesses that have been observed to hold back people from success include impatience, lack of tolerance, anger, poor listening skills, negative body language, lack of concentration and similar problems.

Most people would call these weaknesses trifling and would ignore them. However, a leader who needs to get ahead must gradually overcome these weaknesses. These may look trifling, but they are not. Impatience and lack of tolerance immediately send out the wrong kind of signals. People who lose their temper easily often use foul language and become unreasonable. Those with poor listening skills fail to win over the confidence of others. A negative body language is a sign of inner fears and lack of confidence. With lack of concentration one can easily lose sight of the goal and fail. Through effort one can get over these weaknesses.

The aspiring leader needs to resolve to get rid of the weaknesses one by one. When a person is determined there is nothing that cannot be achieved. Take one weakness every day. For example, if one resolves to be patient, one needs to keep reminding oneself: I will be patient today. Tell your family and friends about it. When you fail they will remind you of your resolution. If you keep practicing the elimination of weaknesses, one each day, you would have handled seven in a week. You can get back to the first one again. Old habits break gradually, and soon you develop new and better habits. Eliminating weaknesses can be as useful as using the strengths to develop effective leadership skills.

Think it over...

Give us, O give us the man who sings at his work! Be his occupation what it may, he is equal to any of those who follow the same pursuit in silent sullenness. He will do more in the same time…he will do it better…he will persevere longer. One is scarcely sensible to fatigue while he marches to music. The very stars are said to make harmony as they revolve in their spheres.

— *Thomas Carlyle*

MAKE WORK FUN

Some leaders appear to work effortlessly while you can see the toll of stress on others. The difference is not in the quantum of work the people are doing, but in the attitude towards work. To some people work is a burden that they need to carry. To a few even working is fun. Working is fun when you do it with great enthusiasm. You do not avoid it, but rather look forward to do it.

Have you ever observed a game of football? Two teams of eleven players each chase a ball trying to kick it into the opposite goal. The game is strenuous, and the players are sturdy. Each player is sweating as they run to kick the ball towards the goal. The game is time-bound. The goals must be scored within the playtime. There is both physical and mental effort. The game also involves technique. Despite the fatigue everyone is happy, and having fun doing whatever they are at. To add to their fun there may be thousands of cheering spectators in the stadium enjoying every movement of the ball. To share the fun, millions may be watching the game on television.

When work is fun to do, one does not feel tired doing it. The level of fatigue is also comparatively low. The work appears to be effortless. With the leader enjoying the work, the team also becomes enthusiastic with the leader, and there is greater fun doing the work at hand.

It may be all right having fun on the football field, but what about the office? Isn't work in the office something serious to do? If everyone was having fun wouldn't the productivity suffer? It is immaterial whether a person is playing football, chess or working in the office. It is not the work that matters. It is the attitude of the worker that is important. Do whatever you need to do in your normal stride. Just add some fun to it. Here are a few ideas that are used in effective workplaces:

- Celebrate your colleague's birthday at teatime. Let everyone know about it. Paste the information on the notice board. The worker will feel important.
- Visit a sick colleague after office hours. He will appreciate your concern.
- Join colleagues on their special occasions, particularly when they need you.
- Use cartoon characters to announce things on the notice board. Use motivational quotations to arouse interest or highlight issues.
- Occasionally organise office parties, picnics, and games after office hours or on a holiday.
- Announce prizes for well-dressed workers, courteous behaviour, dedication beyond duty and other similar things.
- Organise training meetings within the organisation. Make them fun to attend and learn.
- In large business houses workers could be divided into teams, and occasionally the teams could be honoured for special achievements.
- In selling organizations there could be prizes for outstanding salesmen.
- Even within the home many families live like a team sharing responsibilities, and occasionally celebrating special occasions.

When the leader decides to work as though it is great fun, the productivity goes up and the leader is immediately recognised.

STAY FOCUSSED

It is not unusual when most leaders begin with great enthusiasm but midway they lose steam. This is common when a leader is not a self-starter or fails to be self-motivated. Gradually the interest fades away and the work begins to suffer. Some leaders are also willing to accept mediocrity as a norm. To avoid such a situation an effective leader needs to stay focussed on whatever one is doing.

A very common reason for leaders losing focus is their habit of keeping their proposed activities only in the mind, and not writing them down. Even short-term activities are easily forgotten because of new thoughts and situations that seem to draw immediate attention. Since these keep a person busy, one justifies them as valid activities, forgetting that they have lost focus of the things that needed a higher priority of action.

Have you observed that when you go to the super market to purchase the groceries you move through the storage racks viewing all the products that are available, and you can just put it in the handcart. However, you realize that you have missed out on some items only when you return home. This is exactly what happens with the leader who does not note down the things that need to be done. Here are a few ideas that will keep you focussed on what you need to do:

- **Have the goals written down**. There will be several goals before a leader. One cannot possibly remember them all. Even if one has a fantastic

142

memory one may still mix up the priorities. One would need to have long-term goals and short-term goals. These goals will need to be broken into annual goals, quarterly goals, monthly goals and weekly goals. Those who are serious about achieving what they set out to do review the goals regularly, and if there are deviations, corrections are made in time.

- **Work according to a Plan of Action**. An action plan must be made for each of the goals that have been adopted. This would require both macro and micro planning with details of activities that need to be done. The persons involved, the procedures and the deadlines must also be mentioned so that these can be moved to the daily 'to do' list.

- **Have a daily 'to do' list**. Even the weekly goal needs to be broken up into smaller segments. Since there will be other activities and interruptions in the daily routine, the 'to do' list ensures that everything is according to the time frame. It might be preferable to break up the daily 'to do' list into categories like phone calls to be made, people to be contacted, time to check up regular mail and email, filing of documents, reviewing plans, issuing letters, memos and other such items. One could tick each of the tasks as it is completed. If new ones come up, these can be added at the lower end of the list. At the end of the day the list must be reviewed. The items not completed could be moved to a new list for the next day. If an item is not necessary any longer it could be deleted.

- **Review the goals regularly**. Just as the daily list is reviewed at the end of the day, the weekly goals must be reviewed at the end of the week, carrying forward undone tasks. In the same way the monthly, quarterly and annual goals must be reviewed. With goals being reviewed regularly, can the leader lose focus?

- **Maintain a business planner**. A variety of planners are available in the market that can be useful to note down information and keep focussed. It is also possible to design your own planner in a loose-leaf notebook to suit your personal needs.

Staying in focus is very necessary to be an effective leader.

Think it over...

There are two kinds of success. One is the very rare kind that comes to the man who has the power to do what no one else has the power to do. That is genius. But the average man who wins what we call success is not a genius. He is a man who has merely the ordinary qualities that he shares with his fellows, but who has developed those ordinary qualities to a more than ordinary degree.

— *Theodore Roosevelt*

USE POPULAR MANAGEMENT PRINCIPLES

A high level of competition in every field of activity has made it necessary for everyone to know his or her job well, and be efficient. This has been drawing the attention of management gurus, who feel that it is more important to be effective than being efficient. Every leader also desires the same thing. Many concepts have been discussed earlier. Here are a few popular management principles that could be useful to all leaders.

- **Always set goals**. In modern management nothing is done without firm, written goals. Everyone must understand and work to attain the goals.

- **Management by Objectives**. In 1955, Peter Drucker gave the phrase: Management by Objectives. This has changed the mindset of managers all over the world. Setting objectives is to set targets or goals. For convenience, the phrase is abbreviated to MBO.

- **Work to priorities**. It is suggested that every activity must be done in the order of its priority rating. Priorities are best set on the basis of the importance and urgency of the activity. The ABC analysis, which aims at dividing activities into groups, each group called A, B, C and so on, is a popular method of setting priorities. Working to priorities greatly adds to the effectiveness of attaining goals.

- **Adopt the Pareto Time Principle**. Vilfredo Pareto (1848-1923) enunciated this principle. This principle simply states that within any system, some constituent elements yield higher returns than others, with 20 percent of the total elements yielding high returns that produce 80 percent of the work. The other 80 percent of the elements produce 20 percent of the work. This means that on a particular day if we have 10 things to do, if we choose the two most important of the things to do, our productivity would be 80 percent. With some of the other 8 things also done, the productivity would rise proportionately. Some management gurus feel that the proportion should not be 20:80, but 30:70. Much will depend upon the leader's perception of the concept, but it is agreed that it is essential to follow this principle.

- **Prepare lists of things to do**. David Allen has suggested an action management method called Getting Things Done, abbreviated as GTD. This principle suggests that the mind should be emptied of all that needs to be done, and instead it should be noted on paper. This ensures that there is a hard copy before you. The principle is not based upon priorities but on separating different kinds of tasks, and then getting down to what can be done and struck off.

- **Work in harmony with biorhythms**. This principle simply states that with biorhythms varying from one time of the day to the other, one must do difficult tasks at a time when one is on a peak of effectiveness and the routine jobs can be fixed for other times. Although unaware of this principle, many leaders set their daily working schedule accordingly.

- **Use time management techniques**. Time is a very valuable asset and must be used to advantage. Those who use their own time well also respect the time of others.

It is understood that one cannot generalize how different activities must be handled. Everyone is different and would like to handle activities using methods that are in harmony with their temperaments. The important thing is that many people face similar problems and there is a constant effort to seek solutions. These could be useful to others also. The leader needs to look for techniques and methods that can add to one's effectiveness.

Think it over...

My code of life and conduct is simply this; work hard; play to the allowable limit; disregard equally the good and bad opinions of others; never do a friend a dirty trick;...never grow indignant over anything;...live the moment to the utmost of its possibilities;...and be satisfied with life always, but never with oneself.

— *George Jean Nathan*

IMPROVE YOURSELF

The activities of most leaders are restricted to a particular field of work. As one grows in the particular field it becomes necessary to update one's skills and abilities to keep up with the latest developments in science and technology. Knowledge is growing at such a rapid rate that if one ignores to remain updated, one's ideas would soon be obsolete. In everyday life we observe specialists in various fields holding conferences and seminars where papers are presented on the latest developments in that field. Even in the field of business where people learnt more through experience than through other means, the larger business houses now have training departments. The smaller businesses share resources or out-resource facilities for periodical training of staff. Almost in every field one comes across trade journals and magazines. A leader needs to subscribe and read these to remain updated on the latest developments.

The majority of the leaders remain focussed in one field of activity. When they attain success, they strive harder to maintain the position. Since most of the activities are based in the workplace, it is common to find people becoming workaholics. Even when a leader is involved in an activity in social life where one needs to work for a group or the community, the other aspects of life begin to get ignored. This results in a lack of balance in the person's life, and one can observe unhappiness in the home or lack of application at the workplace. A fair balance in the activities at home, the workplace and the society is very important. This makes the leader effective as an individual, with emphasis on the activity of specialization.

One area of life in which most people, both men and women, suffer is personal development. These people will work hard to keep the family happy, fulfil the targets assigned to them at the workplace, and also keep up with the social engagements, but have little or no time for personal fulfilment. This area of life is kept on hold for a suitable period of life when there would be ample free time to give some attention to it. Few people realise that this fulfilment is necessary for attaining personal happiness that is the real purpose of life. People can exist without it, but the life lacks the substance to enrich it. Life is often described as 'empty' or 'hollow'.

If one keeps waiting for that period of time when one would have time to spare, in reality that period never comes. The plain truth is that at no stage in life would a person have time to spare. Everyone has limited time. No one can have more or less of it. If there is an activity for which time is required, one cannot wait for time. The only solution is to manage time better. It will be necessary to find the time for the activity. Therefore, the solution is within the scope of the individual.

Another simple truth that every person must understand is that one cannot postpone personal development indefinitely. Everyone spends the earlier part of life in going to school and college, learning the many skills and abilities that are required in everyday life. That time has really been spent in personal development. However, the moment one steps into adult life, activities within the home, the workplace and the society, why should one totally ignore this aspect as though all that needed to be learnt has been learnt?

Every leader must understand that for each person, life evolves as one goes through one experience after another. Life is dynamic. It is forever changing. To cope with change one needs to be careful about one's health, upgrading of knowledge, building and maintaining relationships within the home, the workplace and the society. One needs to be especially careful about fatigue and stress. To cope with growing pressures there will be need for recreational activities. Besides, one needs growth in one's faith and religious beliefs. To make this possible the leader needs to ensure personal development.

> ## Think it over...
>
> Your morning thoughts may determine your conduct for the day. Optimistic thoughts will make your day bright and productive, while pessimistic thinking will make it dull and wasteful. Face each day cheerfully, smiling and courageously, and it will naturally follow that your work will be a real pleasure and progress will be a delightful accomplishment.
>
> — *William M. Peck*

LIVE ONE DAY AT A TIME

Every leader has a vision. One looks at life on a long-term basis, but lives it on a short-term basis, setting goals according to needs, and attaining them. It is equally important that one lives a balanced life that provides opportunities for personal development, and opportunity for attaining family goals, professional goals and also helps find a place in the society. Time comes from the future and passes into the past. If we have missed some opportunities it is of no use to look at the past with regret. Nor is it useful to live only on hopes that we foresee in the future. God gives us one day at a time to live, and we need to make the best of it.

Every morning, God grants everyone another day that holds promise of many things. It comes to you without distinction of caste, colour or creed. It comes to you without asking you what faith or religion you follow. It does not question your sex or age. It offers you everything that you are willing to work for. Nothing can be attained without making an effort. It is for you to decide where you desire to go as a leader. There is abundance of success and happiness awaiting you. All you need to do is to seek them through persistent effort. When you share your skills and abilities you will be rewarded with greater productivity and success. When you share your love, it will come back manifold reminding you that you have arrived as a true leader in your field.

Bob Gallagher, CEO of Good Will Publishing, emphasizes, "Principled leadership requires the leader to be a teacher, motivator and role model. The virtues of humility, self-discipline and honesty as well as a serious concern for well-being of others are fundamental for principled leadership. It is important to remember that personal integrity is a gift people give to themselves and it can only be surrendered voluntarily. Principled leadership is about service to others. It is about developing relationships with others, either as individuals or as groups, in order to help them move toward truth and justice in a better life."

POINTS TO PONDER

1. To be successful a leader needs to be effective in the field of activity.
2. A leader must be personally motivated to be a self-starter.
3. One's faith in God can be an unending source of inspiration.
4. It is a part of a leader's work to bring about change. It must be correctly understood.
5. To be an effective leader one must put all of one's strengths to use.

6. Everyone needs to get over one's weaknesses.
7. When work is fun it takes little effort to do it.
8. To be effective one must be focussed on the goals.
9. Using popular management principles help make leaders effective.
10. To uphold one's position as a leader one must regularly upgrade skills and abilities, and strive to find personal fulfilment.
11. A house is built brick by brick. Live life one day at a time.

NOTES

....
....
....
....
....
....
....
....
....
....
....
....
....
....
....
....
....
....
....
....
....
....
....
....
....